D1395299

THE
TWELVE
APOSTLES

Tim Pat Coogan is Ireland's best-known historical writer. His 1990 biography of Michael Collins rekindled interest in Collins and his era. He is also the author of *The IRA*; *De Valera: Long Fellow, Long Shadow*; *Wherever Green is Worn*; *The Famine Plot?* and *1916: The Mornings After*.

THE TWELVE APOSTLES

Michael Collins, the Squad and Ireland's Fight for Freedom

TIM PAT COOGAN

HEAD
of ZEUS

First published in 2016 by Head of Zeus Ltd

1 3 5 7 9 10 8 6 4 2

A CIP catalogue record for this book is available from
the British Library.

ISBN (HB) 9781784080136
(E) 9781784080128

Designed and typeset by e-type

Printed and bound by CPI Group (UK) Ltd, Croydon, CR0 4YY

Head of Zeus Ltd
Clerkenwell House
45–47 Clerkenwell Green
London EC1R 0HT

WWW.HEADOFZEUS.COM

For Denis McClean, who suggested the book,
and granddaughters Jessica and Olwen,
who made it possible

Contents

Introduction

Michael Collins addresses a crowd at Skibbereen in his native County Cork, on St Patrick's Day, 27 March 1922.

I T IS MY CONTENTION THAT MICHAEL COLLINS WAS ONE OF the most extraordinary men ever to have been born in Ireland. Collins's remarkable qualities – as a man, a citizen, a commander and strategist – shine through the years; and to me, they gleam all the more brightly in this centenary year of the 1916 Rising. Almost thirty years ago, I wrote my biography of Collins – and he stands at the heart of this book too, because now I want to examine in detail one of his most extraordinary, and certainly most controversial, creations.

This was the Squad, or the Twelve Apostles: the names given to a small undercover unit controlled by Collins which operated in Ireland during the final era of British rule from Dublin Castle. It is crucial to note that the Apostles were by no means superbly resourced – indeed, the opposite is the case: the unit was only ever lightly armed: the original .38 pistols held by its members were eventually swapped for rather more powerful but still essentially modest .45 revolvers – and in such improbable fashion, these individuals took on the forces of a state that was equipped lavishly with artillery, machine guns, rifles and tanks. The real firepower of the Twelve Apostles, however, originated elsewhere, from sources that the state could neither control nor eliminate: from widespread public support among the Irish in Ireland and abroad (especially in the United States); from sheer idealism; and from an enormously potent intelligence-gathering operation that was also masterminded and run by Collins himself.

Collins was a difficult man. He let off steam by wild bouts of furniture-smashing and wrestling matches. He was given to practical jokes that were not all that funny. He had a volcanic temper, and he could be bullying. Yet he was the Squad's alpha and omega; the story begins and ends with this fascinating and controversial character. One man's freedom fighter is, after all, another man's terrorist – and nobody in modern Irish history encapsulates this slogan more fully than Collins, who can well be described as both a freedom fighter and a terrorist.

Indeed, Michael Collins was a walking contradiction of a man. He was both an idealist and a realist, with the two conflicting parts fused together by his genius and his incredible energy, his ruthlessness and his compassion. His idealism had taken him into Dublin's General Post Office during the 1916 Rising, but the first of his reasons for forming the Squad is contained in recollections following this traumatic week in Dublin. He told his friend Kevin O'Brien (as I record in my biography *Michael Collins*) that:

It is so easy to fault the actions of others when their particular actions have resulted in defeat. I want to be quite fair about this – The Easter Rising – and say how much I admired the men in the ranks and the womenfolk thus engaged. But at the same time – as it must appear to others

6

also – the actions of the leaders should not pass without comment.

They have died nobly at the hands of the firing squads. So much I grant. But I do not think The Rising week was an appropriate time for the issue of Memoranda couched in poetic phrase, nor of actions worked out in a similar fashion. Looking at it from the inside (I was in the GPO), it had the air of a Greek tragedy about it, the illusion being more or less completed with the aforementioned memoranda. Of Pearse and Connolly I admire the latter the most. Connolly was a realist, Pearse the direct opposite. There was an air of earthy directness about Connolly. It impressed me. I would have followed him through hell, had such action been necessary. But I honestly doubt so much if I would have followed Pearse – not without some thought anyway. I think chiefly of Tom Clarke and Mac Diarmada. Both built on the best foundations. Ireland will not see another Seán Mac Diarmada. These are sharp reflections. On the whole I think the Rising was bungled terribly, costing many a good life. It seemed at first to be well organised, but afterwards became subject to panic decisions and a great lack of very essential organisation and cooperation.

Collins, then, had not only participated in great and stirring events. He had watched too – and he had learned. He had made up his mind that in the new round of fighting, not merely should that round not be bungled – it must be a *new* form of resistance. There was to be no more 'static warfare' such as had been witnessed across Dublin during the Rising, consisting as it did of taking a strong point and holding on gallantly until superior numbers and firepower inevitably crushed the insurgents. This was certainly stirring to behold and support – but it was doomed to fail.

In addition, Collins had witnessed the political detectives going about the room full of captured prisoners in Richmond barracks in Dublin, identifying the rebel leaders for the British Army – and for the firing squads. It was a grim lesson in the importance of intelligence, of the political police or 'G-Men', and of the machinery of repression that held the country – and this was only underlined further for him when an intelligence officer in Dublin Castle, Edward – Ned – Broy, smuggled him into Brunswick Street police station one evening. Collins spent a crucial night here sifting through the police records which demonstrated how the collection of political intelligence was an essential tool in the maintenance of British control. Later, his thinking and planning would justify the ruthless means by which he put an end to that control.

In an interview with me, Vincent (Vinnie) Byrne – one of the Squad's most celebrated members – told me:

We were all young: 20–21. We never thought we would win or lose. We just wanted to have a go. We would go out in pairs, walk up to the target and do it, then split. You wouldn't be nervous while you would be waiting to plug him, but you would imagine everyone was looking into your face. On a typical job we would use about eight, including the backup. Nobody got in our way. One of us would knock him over with the first shot, and the other would finish him off with a shot to the head. Collins was a marvel. If he hadn't done the work he did, we would still be under Britain. Informers and drink would have taken care of us, but our movement was temperate. Collins would meet us from time to time and say, *you're doing great work, lads.* There was no formality about him. I remember after the Irish government was set up, I was on guard duty at Government Buildings, and he was Commander in Chief. He saw me and came over to me and put his arm around me and said, *How are you going on, Vinny?*

And his colleague and friend Frank Thornton summed Collins up thus:

Mick Collins was the ideal soldier to lead men during a revolution such as we were going through and I think all and sundry whether they subsequently fought against him in the civil war or not who had close contact with him, must admit that he was the one bright star that all the fighting men looked to for guidance and advice.

In addition, the story of Collins and the evolution of his reputation has been marked, shaped and at times stunted by the context against which twentieth-century Irish history unfolded. For decades after Collins's death (in August 1922, at the age of thirty-one), his most formidable adversary held power in

Ireland – and Éamon de Valera saw to it that his own reputation was extolled, most thoroughly, and to the detriment of Collins and his legacy. Indeed, a cross erected over Collins's grave by his brother Johnny at Glasnevin Cemetery was only permitted on a reduced scale and to a design sanctioned by de Valera himself; and Collins's name was excised from an official government handbook produced on the fiftieth anniversary of the 1916 Rising.

So long as de Valera's palsied hands gripped the reins of power, moreover, representatives of the Irish Army, of which Collins was the first Commander-in-Chief and within the ranks of which Collins's memory was held in the highest regard, were not permitted to attend the annual commemoration at the place where he was killed, Béal na Bláth in West Cork. Indeed, it was not until 1990 and the centenary of Collins's birth (when incidentally, I had the honour of delivering the commemorative oration), that an Irish Taoiseach permitted Irish Army personnel to attend.

This mean-spirited and ungenerous treatment at home did not, however, affect Collins's reputation as a guerrilla leader abroad. Take the example of one of the most ruthless and successful guerrilla movements of the twentieth century, which led eventually to the creation of the state of Israel in what had been the British Mandate of Palestine. The Jewish leader Yitzhak Shamir both studied the methods of Michael Collins, and used the code name Michael as his own *nom de guerre*. And in the state of Israel which Shamir helped to form, I was made aware of a guilty foreboding on the part of those Israeli citizens who knew their history, that one day the Arabs too might produce a Michael Collins – and that if they did, there would not be a supermarket left standing in Israel.

During his lifetime too, there was no shortage of observers who knew exactly what Collins was capable of achieving, and what he might do with his energy and talents – and in the years that followed his death, many individuals were more than prepared to learn from Collins and from the methods he deployed. Imitation is, after all, the sincerest form of flattery – and his British adversaries paid him the supreme compliment of importing Collins's tactics and adopting them in their own covert military operations. When the Special Operations Executive (SOE) – sometimes known as 'Churchill's toy shop' – was established at the onset of the Second World War, Winston Churchill envisaged the force 'setting Europe ablaze' through the use of such distinctly Collins-esque methods as assassination and sabotage.

The SOE was tutored in Collins-patented methods by Major General Sir Colin Gubbins, a prime mover in the British forces of the time, who described his experience of service in the Ireland of the 1920s as 'being shot at from behind hedges by men in trilbies and mackintoshes and not being allowed to shoot back'. Irish survivors of the Anglo-Irish War, particularly wounded ones, were left in some puzzlement as to where the bullets did come from. But there is no mystery about the fact that in later years, Gubbins would lecture the SOE on the lessons of his Irish service, warning them in particular to leave no documentation behind them and commit as much as possible to memory. Gubbins knew what he was talking about: as I will discuss in the following pages, Collins and the IRA devoted much time and energy to the capture of British documents; and, towards the end of the conflict, the British benefited from the capture of pieces of Collins's own paper trail.

Gubbins drew many of his recruits from the British public school system – but the individuals who comprised Collins's elite, or Twelve Apostles, were members of a rather different tribe. They were largely working-class men and women whom he sculpted into a hidden army that drove a spear into the heart of an empire. He commanded them by force of personality, for in addition to the difficult and tempestuous personality I have mentioned above, Collins possessed something – one might call it the X Factor – that explains more than a thousand military manuals ever could how he wielded that empire-wounding spear. In the words of Frank O'Connor, whose biography *The Big Fellow* (1937) allows the sheer humanity of this public figure to shine through, Collins took:

> the simplest men, men to whom no man in the world had ever attached importance to, and made them feel that the smallest task they performed was a matter of life and death. Before him, after him, none could give them the same sense of responsibility, and their devotion to him was no greater than his to them.

As for the members whom he controlled and commanded: these individuals performed dark and brutal deeds, and when the Anglo-Irish War was over some of them performed even darker ones. War, after all, can never be sloughed off: on the contrary, it has a habit of affecting the winners just as much as the losers. Yet this small band captured the imagination of large swathes of the Irish public. The idea that the Lilliputians, after centuries of conquest, could at last strike back successfully against an enormously stronger foe: this sense overlaid the grimmer realities of war and strife with a patina of romance that has still not faded – even if contemporary Irish attitudes towards militarism generally tend to be more critical and analytical than of yore.

Change is effected, and history made, by a combination of will and circumstances. Collins had the will: and in the circumstances of his day he and the Squad altered the course of Irish history. The world has changed much in the century since Collins and his Apostles took on the authority of the British state in Ireland. The echoes of the bombings and shootings in Northern Ireland have largely died away since the conclusion of the Good Friday Agreement in 1998: and as we have lately seen, the Republic's decision-takers have deemed it safe to allow the people to take ownership of the commemoration of the centenary of the Easter Rising – unfettered by doubts and fears of what reaction this might elicit from either Conservatives at Westminster or Unionists in Ulster. Michael Collins and his Apostles played a vivid and, in the end, decisive, role in the history of the years that we are now committed to remembering. I want to turn now to their story.

CHAPTER ONE

A Fatal Policy

The burnt-out shell of the Dublin General Post Office after the 1916 Easter Rising.

HOW DID A TINY SQUAD OF MEN, THEIR NUMBER INDICATED by their nickname 'The Twelve Apostles', come to change Irish history? The answer is born out of the story of Ireland and of its relationship with England and Britain: and its origins as a result reach back into the distant past. One beginning – although there are many others from which to choose – lies in the sixteenth century, when the Tudor monarchs set about the reconquest of an Ireland that had long been drifting out of the English sphere of influence. The final phase of this reconquest, the Elizabethan wars of the 1590s, began the process of de-Gaelicising the province of Ulster, until that point the region of Ireland most removed from English control. This process was accelerated with the Plantation of Ulster instituted by the first Stuart king, James I, in the opening years of the seventeenth century. The Plantation saw the removal of the native Catholic Irish from their lands and their replacement with Anglican settlers from England and Presbyterians from the Scottish lowlands. In the decades that followed, the Plantation proceeded – haltingly and more slowly than its architects would have liked, and accompanied by bouts of bloody violence, as Protestant farmers furrowed Catholic lands with, as it were, one hand on the musket, and the other on the plough.

It was in such thoroughly tilled soil that certain political operatives were able, from time to time, to raise rich crops. Let us leap forward in time now, to the late nineteenth century – and to one such operative: the British Conservative politician Randolph Churchill, who sowed seeds of dissension in Ireland by his policy of what he termed 'playing the Orange card'. Churchill was fond of his apothegms: another such was his declaration that 'Ulster will fight and Ulster will be right', made to an appreciative audience at the Ulster Hall in Belfast in February 1886. Churchill had a specific political agenda: to deploy the anti-Catholic Unionism of Ulster's Protestant community as a weapon in domestic British politics. It was an agenda based entirely on expediency, for Churchill had no love for the Unionists of Ulster; indeed, he was on record as referring to them as 'those foul Ulster Tories [who] have always ruined our party'.

Churchill, indeed, was motivated by the specific political context of the day. In early 1886, the Tories were out of office in London – and likely to stay that way so long as Prime Minister William Gladstone led the Liberal Party. Gladstone was now, after years of opposition to the measure, a firm proponent of Home Rule for Ireland – a proponent, that is, for a measure of political self-rule that had been removed from Ireland by the Act of Union of 1800. The arithmetic of the House of Commons, and the political pressure applied by the Irish Parliamentary Party led by Charles Stewart Parnell, had now nudged the Prime Minister to support the notion – and for the first time it appeared as though Home Rule might actually be granted by Westminster.

It was at this crucial juncture, so laced with myriad possibilities for the future of Anglo-Irish relationships, and of Catholic–Protestant relationships within Ireland, that Randolph Churchill stepped into the fray. He declared that if Gladstone achieved Home Rule, the way to defeat him was to play the Orange card. 'Pray God,' he said, 'that it will turn out an ace, not a deuce.' The Orange card policy consisted of incitement to hatred – and crossing to Belfast, Churchill encapsulated it, to a roaring Orange audience (on 23 February, 1886) with the slogan which explains why to this day, Ulster's six north-eastern counties form part of the United Kingdom: 'Ulster will fight and Ulster will be right'. Churchill's rhetoric so inflamed Belfast Protestants that they fell on Catholic homes and places of employment, burning, rioting and re-igniting old sectarian fears so completely that at the time of writing they have yet to fully die away. The Orange Card, then, did turn out to be a triumphant ace for the Conservatives. Home Rule was stalled within the Commons, the Liberal Party split under the strain, the Gladstone administration of 1886 fell – and personal scandal felled Parnell himself, who died in 1891 with his party and the dream of Home Rule in tatters and for a generation removed beyond reach.

Slowly and painfully, however, Parnell's successor John Redmond succeeded in putting the riven Irish Parliamentary Party together again – and by 1912, the parliamentary arithmetic once more suggested that the attainment of Home Rule was a possibility. Once again, a Liberal government – this time led by Herbert Asquith – was in office, and once again it was dependent on the votes of a renewed and emboldened Irish Parliamentary Party. Moreover, Irish lobbying had contributed to a crucial reform having being secured: the removal by means of the Parliament Act of the veto on House of Commons legislation by the Conservative-dominated House of Lords. For decades, this veto had been used to frustrate the passage of Home Rule Bills into law – but now Redmond, after years of painstaking constitutional work putting together what had been broken in the fall of Parnell, appeared to be on the brink of success.

It is important to note that Asquith's proposals for Home Rule were hardly revolutionary. They conformed to the classical colonial formula of 'We will appear to give you freedom, but in reality tell you how to use it.' Dublin was to get a parliament, but in reality not much else. This parliament was envisaged as consisting of the king, a Senate and a House of Commons. The head of the Irish Executive was envisaged as being not an elected Irish parliamentarian, but a London-appointed Lord Lieutenant who in turn was to appoint Ministers and the membership of the Senate and judiciary. In addition, London would retain control over taxation, foreign relations, trade outside Ireland, and the army and navy; and would in addition retain the power to alter or repeal any act of the Dublin parliament.

Modest these reforms undoubtedly were – yet they were not modest enough for the British Conservative Party, which reacted to the introduction of these proposals as though anarchy had been released upon the world. Randolph Churchill was now gone from the scene – he died in 1895 – but once more his Tory heirs swiftly played the Orange card. For example, speaking at Blenheim Palace in the summer of 1912, at a vicious time when 'Belfast confetti' (rivets) rained down on Catholic workers as the Unionists reacted to Home Rule proposals by driving thousands of Catholics out of the Belfast shipyards, the Conservative leader Andrew Bonar Law spoke words that might have been written by Randolph Churchill himself. He told his Unionist audience that, regardless of their tactics and the lengths to which they might choose to go in order to combat the threat of Home Rule, they would be supported by the Conservative Party. 'There are stronger things than parliamentary majorities,' this alleged democrat told his listeners – and they roared their approval. Two months later, in September 1912, hundreds of thousands of Ulstermen (the women had their own document) signed the Ulster Covenant, pledging resistance by:

> using all means which may be found necessary to defeat the present conspiracy to set up a Home Rule Parliament in Ireland. And in the event of such a Parliament being forced upon us, we further solemnly and mutually pledge ourselves to resist its authority.

Serious measures were taken to put flesh on the bones of this declaration of rebellion. The importation of arms had for some months become a feature on the Ulster political landscape: the Ulster Volunteers militia force paraded and drilled openly; and Protestant justices of the peace issued licenses which ostensibly allowed the Volunteers to carry arms – even though the law of the land said otherwise. By September of the following year, Ulster was being convulsed by a series of anti-Home Rule meetings and parades. The *de facto* Unionist leader, Edward Carson, announced that, should Home Rule become law, he and the Unionist leadership would establish a government to take over the province; neither Carson nor his Conservative allies, in other words, were now making any pretence of being bound by the rule of law. In a particularly inflammatory speech delivered at Newry on 7 September 1913, Carson (who was a King's Counsel) said of the proposed Ulster government:

> I am told it will be illegal. Of course it will. Drilling is illegal [...] the Volunteers are illegal and the Government knew they are illegal and the Government does not interfere with them [...] Don't be afraid of illegalities.

F. E. Smith, later to become Lord Chancellor, chimed in on this treasonable chorus on behalf of the Conservatives: he told an audience at Ballyclare in County Antrim on 20 September that the moment Home Rule became law, the Conservative leadership would say to its followers: 'To your tents, O Israel!' Smith told his listeners that the Conservatives were ready to 'risk the collapse of the whole body politic to prevent this monstrous crime'.

Four days later, the Unionists spawned the first Provisionals of the century, as the Ulster Unionist Council morphed itself into the Central Authority of the Provisional Government of

Ulster, with Carson as its Chairman. Other members included the Duke of Abercorn (who held estates in County Tyrone), the enormously influential Lord Londonderry (whose family seat was at Mount Stewart in County Down), and Sir James Craig (who was destined to become the first Prime Minister of the future Northern Ireland). A fund of £1 million to provide for the widows and orphans created by any war which might follow this step was quickly established in both Ireland and Britain. Sir Henry Wilson, later Field Marshal and Chief of the Imperial General Staff, was particularly active in the ranks of the prominent British generals who offered these Provisionals their services in the event of war. (Subsequently, when the partition of Ireland had become a reality, Sir Henry would make good on his promise: he acted as security advisor to Sir James Craig, and was responsible for organising loyalist death squads. As we shall see, this was an activity which would ultimately lead to his assassination.)

It is hardly necessary at this stage to remind readers that while this tumult was ongoing in Ireland, in the world outside, a greater conflagration was approaching. In spite of this looming world war, however, the Conservative-Unionist alliance protest movement, most remarkably, elicited what was in effect a mutiny amongst the officers stationed in the Curragh, the principal British military garrison in Ireland. The army corps there under General Gough told the British government that they would not move against Ulster to enforce Home Rule. This was in March 1914. A month later the army's policy, and that of the navy, was underscored at Larne, when, under the averted gaze of both the senior services and of the police, the Orangemen landed and distributed a cargo of German weaponry without a hand being raised to stop them. Before the summer was out, the United Kingdom and Germany were at war.

The German willingness to go to war that summer, indeed, is thought by some historians to have been influenced by this specific and highly unusual context; and by advice to the Kaiser that Britain would surely not dare to fight a European war when a civil war was apparently threatening. The Unionist historian A. T. Q. Stewart, in his commendably objective *The Ulster Crisis*, describes how German decision-makers thought of the Unionists as 'the Kaiser's Irish Friends'. Nor was this advice wholly unfounded. In January 1913, for example, Carson moved a motion in the House of Commons to exclude 'Ulster' from the provisions of the Home Rule Bill. By now, practically speaking, 'Ulster', in the minds of some Unionist leaders, was coming to mean in practice the present six counties of Northern Ireland, rather than the nine counties which constitute the ancient province of Ulster. The reasoning had everything to do with cold demographic arithmetic: the Unionist establishment admitted privately that it could not control the full nine counties of Ulster because of the inconvenient presence there of so many Catholics.

Now, moving his exclusion motion, Carson stated candidly that rather than be ruled by Irish Nationalists the Unionists would 'prefer to accept the government of a foreign country'. In fact, Carson had lunched with Kaiser Wilhelm II in Hamburg a year before war was declared: and a spate of allegedly well-founded rumours about German support broke out amongst Unionists. In November 1913, the *Irish Churchman* – a respected Protestant journal – published what was widely believed to have been agreed at that Hamburg lunch:

> We have the offer of aid from a powerful continental monarch who, if Home Rule is forced on the Protestants of Ireland, is prepared to send an army sufficient to release England of any further trouble in Ireland by attaching it to his dominion [...] And should our King sign the Home Rule bill, the Protestants of Ireland will welcome this continental deliverer as their forefathers under similar circumstances did once before [a reference to the invitation to William of Orange in 1688].

The result of such domestic tension was almost inevitable. The government moved to appease Carson and the Unionists of Ulster: in September 1914, when the Home Rule Bill did actually pass through the House of Commons and into law, it was suspended for the duration of the war. The threat of civil conflict now receded – but for John Redmond's constitutional Home Rule movement in Ireland, this was a blow from which it would never recover. The object of Conservative policy in reality, of course, had never been simply to give aid and succour to the Unionists, but rather to destabilise and if possible to overthrow the Liberal government. Nevertheless, the Conservative and Unionist threat to use force to frustrate the implementation of the democratically expressed wishes of a majority of the British and Irish people fairly deserves to be recognised as the first major success for fascist tactics in twentieth-century Europe. As far as Nationalist Ireland was concerned, of course, many people watched the tactics of Carson, the Unionists and the Conservative Party, and learned from them – and among these observers was Michael Collins.

There is a saying in Irish: *Uisce faoi thalamh*. This literally translates as 'water under the ground' – but it is generally taken to mean 'secret activity'. And indeed, there was a good deal of secret activity in Ireland in these years, and not only in Ulster. Best remembered, perhaps, is the secret organisation called the Irish Republican Brotherhood (IRB), which had been founded in the aftermath of the Famine years to overthrow British rule in Ireland; its members were popularly known as the Fenians, after the legendary Irish equivalent of the Samurai. Away from the limelight, the once moribund IRB had used these tense pre-war years to restructure and quietly infiltrate the myriad of Irish Nationalist organisations blossoming into life in the so-called Celtic Revival. This era saw the political energies of Ireland that had been diffused by the fall of Parnell diverted into cultural and sporting outlets such as the Gaelic League, Gaelic Athletic Association and Abbey Theatre, which had been established by Augusta Gregory and W. B. Yeats – and it was from this welter of cultural and political nationalism that the IRB selected the weapon it required for rebellion.

In 1913, the Gaelic scholar Eoin MacNeill wrote an article in the journal of the Gaelic League, *An Claíomh Solais* (The Bright

Sword). MacNeill advocated that a force of Irish Volunteers be established to counter the attempts by the Conservatives to make force the ultimate arbiter of Home Rule. The formation of the Ulster Volunteers gave the proposal an immediate appeal in the eyes of Nationalists all over the country, and thousands of young men joined the new force. The women's auxiliary force Cumann na mBan and the radical Inghinidhe na hÉireann (Daughters of Ireland) organisation also received considerable popular support – and indeed, women would play a key role in the struggle that lay ahead.

MacNeill had intended the Volunteers to be a purely defensive force to be used solely to defend Home Rule, should its opponents use force to prevent its introduction. Unknown to him, however, the IRB had very efficiently infiltrated the Volunteers and secured positions of leadership within the movement. In these years, the Brotherhood recruited such energetic members as the youthful Collins; and Pádraig Pearse, a barrister, orator, poet and propagandist, who declared openly that he found the spectacle of an Orangeman with a rifle less ridiculous than that of a Nationalist without one.

As was the case with the UVF, the Volunteers were armed, though – bereft of sponsors as powerful as the British Conservative Party – to a far lesser extent. On the eve of war, however, arms *were* imported – and in the meantime, another force was also stirring, drilling, threatening rebellion – and proclaiming that they served neither King nor Kaiser, but only Ireland. This was the Irish Citizen Army founded in Dublin by James Connolly – initially as a means of defending the workers against police brutality in the Great Lockout of 1913. The workers had been defeated in this instance by the employers led by William Martin Murphy, proprietor of the *Irish Independent*; and had been readmitted to their jobs after signing a promise not to join a trade union. In the aftermath of the Lockout, Connolly and his ally Constance Markievicz – herself a scion of an established Anglo-Irish family – continued to use the Citizen Army to drill and actively prepare for armed struggle. And so, fearing that he might bring the authorities down on them prematurely, the IRB co-opted Connolly into the leadership of the movement.

Thomas Clarke was the principal figure in the IRB, and a profoundly influential figure in the evolution of Irish Nationalist philosophy in this period. Clarke had served fifteen years' penal servitude for his part, under the alias of Henry Wilson, in the Fenian dynamiting campaign in Britain in the 1880s. Some of this period had been spent in solitary confinement, during which time he kept himself sane by means that included cutting a button from his uniform and then spending hours on his hands and knees searching for it in the darkness of his cell. Clarke's reputation was such that John Redmond had campaigned vigorously for his release, saying on one occasion that 'Wilson is a man of whom no words of praise could be too high. I have learned in my many visits to Portland [Jail] for five years to love, honour and respect Henry Wilson. I have seen day after day how his brave spirit was keeping him alive [...] I have seen year after year the fading away of his physical strength.' The irony is, of course, that Clarke would ultimately prove to be the main architect of Redmond's political destruction.

On completion of his sentence, Clarke went to the United States with the authorities still not realising that the name Wilson by which he was known was a *nom de guerre*. In America, Clarke married Kathleen Daly, a member of a leading Limerick Fenian family, and the Clarkes attained a modest prosperity, acquiring some property including two small farms. Clarke's period in America was relatively quiet – and yet it encapsulates the growing influence of the United States in general, and the vast Irish diaspora in America in particular, in Irish affairs. Irish America was able to provide a degree of political leverage and send a flow of dollars east across the Atlantic: and both Nationalist Ireland and the British government were aware of the fact. Historically when the Irish had risen in rebellion, the British were able to ring the island with ships to quell foreign intervention and then use their superior military strength on the island to snuff out what was termed 'disaffection' – a favourite British term for Irish unrest. But increasingly now, there was a loud, often uncoordinated, but never less than powerful force to be reckoned with – and one beyond the reach of the British army or navy.

In 1907, the Clarkes relinquished their moderately prosperous American life to return to Dublin, where Thomas Clarke opened a tobacconist and newsagent on Parnell Street. The shop became in due course a gathering place for younger IRB men, particularly Seán Mac Diarmada, who in public became general manager of the IRB's *Irish Freedom* newspaper, and in private acted as the brotherhood's principal organiser. This was a society increasingly influenced by Clarke – and with British attention fixed on the European war, it was also a faction now bent on seizing the opportunity to foment a revolt in Ireland itself.

As the Conservative-sponsored Unionist revolt gathered force, the Germans extended their dubious friendship to the Nationalist side of the argument also. Prior to the outbreak of the First World War, a leading IRB figure, Joseph Plunkett, had visited Germany and received assurances that German aid would be forthcoming. After war had actually broken out, the world-renowned humanitarian Roger Casement also visited Germany to follow up on these promises, and to raise a spirit of rebellion among those Irish-born British soldiers who had been captured in Flanders and elsewhere, and who were now being held as prisoners of war in Germany itself. These attempts failed; moreover, Casement also failed to secure the expected supply of assistance in the form of artillery and German officers – and now he sought to delay or cancel an uprising that he knew could not possibly succeed. To no avail: Casement returned to Ireland on board a German submarine, and was arrested when he was put ashore on the County Kerry coast. He would presently pay for his actions with his life.

Casement's doubts were well founded, of course – but the material point is that the IRB leadership had decided that the Rising must go ahead. Not because they thought it would succeed, even with German help, but for three other main reasons: one, to resist Conscription into the British Army, should an attempt be made by the government to enforce it on Ireland; two, because it was felt that the very act of rebellion would gain public sympathy within Ireland and in America; and three, that by rising and declaring a republic, Ireland would secure a place at the Peace Conference which would inevitably follow the Great War's ending.

Michael Collins had spent the decade before the Easter Rising living and working in London. Now, alerted by Sam Maguire (the leader of the IRB in Britain) that something was afoot, Collins was one of fifteen IRB men who returned to Ireland to take part in the planned rebellion. He took up employment as a financial advisor to Joseph Plunkett's wealthy parents in Kimmage, south Dublin – where his financial activities took second place to rifle practice and bomb making. It was here that Joseph Plunkett advised him to read G. K. Chesterton's thriller *The Man Who Was Thursday*. From this work, Collins developed one of the guiding principles of his subsequent revolutionary career: he never thought of himself as being 'on the run': rather, he hid in plain sight, and he refused to wear a disguise. He understood, in other words, that if he didn't look as though he were on the run, it was much less likely that anyone would pursue him or seek him out.

On Easter Monday, 24 April 1916, Collins dressed in his Volunteer uniform, and set forth. His uniform was immaculate, so much so that it drew jeers and sarcasm from the generally shabby-looking rank-and-file fellow Volunteers. His role on the day was to act as *aide de camp* to Joseph Plunkett, who was recuperating from an operation, but who had left his sickbed just the same to join the rebellion. As he, Casement and many others knew, however, the Rising itself had little chance of succeeding – and now circumstances rendered success even less likely. On its eve, MacNeill, discovering. what the IRB had planned for the following day, issued a countermanding order which caused many Volunteers to stay at home. The force had already suffered a major split following a call by Redmond to support the British war effort: the largest section of the Volunteers had answered Redmond's entreaty, leaving only a small minority who refused the British call to arms. Now, following MacNeill's action, only a rump of a rump marched out to seize a number of strategic points around Dublin that Easter Monday. The rebels' first, and best remembered, action was to take the General Post Office, where Pearse read a Proclamation declaring an Irish Republic and promising to cherish all the children of the nation equally. The text of the Proclamation subsequently became the *Magna Carta* of Irish Nationalists.

POBLACHT NA hÉIREANN
THE PROVISIONAL GOVERNMENT OF THE IRISH
REPUBLIC TO THE PEOPLE OF IRELAND

IRISHMEN AND IRISHWOMEN:
In the name of God and of the dead generations from which she receives her old tradition of nationhood, Ireland, through us, summons her children to her flag and strikes for her freedom.

Having organised and trained her manhood through her secret revolutionary organisation, the Irish Republican Brotherhood, and through her open military organisations, the Irish Volunteers and the Irish Citizen Army, having patiently perfected her discipline, having resolutely waited for the right moment to reveal itself, she now seizes that moment, and supported by her exiled children in America and by gallant allies in Europe, but relying in the first on her own strength, she strikes in full confidence of victory.

We declare the right of the people of Ireland to the ownership of Ireland and to the unfettered control of Irish destinies, to be sovereign and indefeasible. The long usurpation of that right by a foreign people and government has not extinguished the right, nor can it ever be extinguished except by the destruction of the Irish people. In every generation the Irish people have asserted their right to national freedom and sovereignty; six times during the past three hundred years they have asserted it in arms. Standing on that fundamental right and again asserting it in arms in the face of the world, we hereby proclaim the Irish Republic as a Sovereign Independent State, and we pledge our lives and the lives of our comrades in arms to the cause of its freedom, of its welfare, and of its exaltation among the nations.

The Irish Republic is entitled to, and hereby claims, the allegiance of every Irishman and Irishwoman. The Republic guarantees religious and civil liberty, equal rights and equal opportunities to all its citizens, and declares its resolve to pursue the happiness and prosperity of the whole nation and of all its parts, cherishing all of the children of the nation equally, and oblivious of the differences carefully fostered by an alien Government, which have divided a minority from the majority in the past.

Until our arms have brought the opportune moment for the establishment of a permanent National Government, representative of the whole people of Ireland and elected by the suffrages of all her men and women, the Provisional Government, hereby constituted, will administer the civil and military affairs of the Republic in trust for the people.

We place the cause of the Irish Republic under the protection of the Most High God, Whose blessing we invoke upon our arms, and we pray that no one who serves that cause will dishonour it by cowardice, inhumanity, or rapine. In this supreme hour the Irish nation must, by its valour and discipline, and by the readiness of its children to sacrifice themselves for the common good, prove itself worthy of the august destiny to which it is called.

Signed on behalf of the Provisional Government:

THOMAS J. CLARKE

SEAN Mac DIARMADA   THOMAS MacDONAGH

P. H. PEARSE   EAMONN CEANNT

JAMES CONNOLLY   JOSEPH PLUNKETT

Although the British had only about 1200 troops in Dublin when the Rising broke out, this rose within a day to approximately 5000 as reinforcements were brought in from Belfast and from Britain. Heavy artillery was positioned within the grounds of Trinity College, and fired too from a gunboat moored on the river Liffey close to city-centre rebel strongholds. The rebels held out for almost a week, encircled by an ever-growing ring of well-armed soldiers and bombarded by artillery fire which would leave much of central Dublin in ruins. Initially this destruction and loss of life brought a torrent of abuse about the rebels' heads: the Anglican Archbishop of Dublin, for example, led a chorus of demands for punishment; and the Catholic Hierarchy refused a church-door collection for the Rising's victims lest it be taken that they supported what had happened. This chorus of blame lasted for some weeks – with a final salvo from the *Irish Independent*'s leader column, which in effect called for James Connolly's execution.

*

The aftermath of the Rising created a particular personal bitterness for Collins that he would expunge some years later. After the surrender, the GPO prisoners, including Thomas Clarke, were herded together on a grassy patch behind the Rotunda Hospital: here, they lay out in the open, with no shelter or dignity, and were forced to relieve themselves where they lay. Apart from his age (he was now fifty-eight), Clarke was in pain from a bullet wound in his elbow which he had accidently sustained during pistol practice before the Rising. Throughout the night, Collins did what he could to keep Clarke warm by wrapping his arms around him. One of the British officers supervising the prisoners, a Captain Lee Wilson, apparently realising Clarke's importance, had him stripped and paraded naked in front of some of the nurses looking out from the windows of the Rotunda. That action was to cost him his life: Collins had him shot a few years later.*

Indeed, Collins understood now that the conflict to come was to be a new type of war – and an event at Dublin's Richmond Barracks in the aftermath of the surrender helped him both to choose the targets and to begin to think in terms of a squad of operatives that would, in time, become the Twelve Apostles. While the prisoners were held at the barracks, the G-Men – detectives from the political police – went through the prisoners selecting their leaders for execution. With that extraordinary facility for skirting danger that would later contribute so much to the legend of this man, Collins escaped the attentions of the G-man screening his section. Someone called out his name from the far end of the large room: he got up to see who it was – and sat down simply and neatly in a corner of the room that had already been screened. Thus the British missed, at this early stage, the Rising's most dangerous survivor.

---

* The subsequent kindness of the Jesuits to Captain Lee Wilson's wife, Dr Marie Lee Wilson, resulted in the gifting to the Irish nation of a near priceless Caravaggio painting, the eerily appropriate *The Taking of Christ*, showing Roman soldiers capturing Christ at the moment of the Judas kiss. Ms Wilson, not knowing its value, had given the painting to the Jesuits out of gratitude to her friend, Fr. Finlay SJ, who, following her husband's death, had helped her through a breakdown from which she never fully recovered. When the identity of the painter was discovered decades later, the Jesuits presented the painting to the National Gallery of Ireland.

Executions followed these screenings: sixteen in all. Fifteen of them were men who had taken part in the Rising – and these died before firing squads. The sixteenth was of course Casement, who was hanged at Pentonville Jail in London on 3 August 1916. The list of the executed included all the seven signatories of the Proclamation, plus Edward Daly, a brother of Kathleen Clarke; others, including Markievicz and the American-born Éamon de Valera, who had commanded, not very efficiently, a battalion at Boland's Mill – were spared. The executions were spread out over a number of days: the last to die was James Connolly, who was suffering so badly from a bullet wound in the ankle that he had to be given morphine to sleep and strapped into a chair to be shot.

It is worth pausing at this moment to offer a vignette on the behaviour of de Valera, who would emerge intact and with a remarkably burnished reputation from the events of Easter 1916. He was a married man with, at this point, five children – and his responsibilities bore heavily on him during the fighting, to such an extent that he suffered a form of nervous collapse. He went for several days without sleep, until his men finally persuaded him to get some rest in a railway carriage on a siding in the nearby Westland Row station. De Valera himself never mentioned this nervous episode at the time: but nearly fifty years later he did reveal that he thought he had died and gone to heaven; and that when he woke, the carriage was filled with angels and baskets of fruit flying through space. Eventually he realised that these 'angels' were made of plaster of Paris! – for he was in the carriage used to take members of the Royal Family on their rail journeys.

However distraught he may or may not have been, de Valera's instinct for self-preservation certainly never deserted him. His command post never came under direct attack, but the fighting at his main outpost, several hundred yards away at Mount Street Bridge, was ferocious. The casualties sustained in this area by the British comprised half of the total casualties of the Rising – a fact that would later burnish de Valera's reputation considerably. Yet, when the desperate Mount Street rebels sought reinforcements, their leader refused them. As Max Caulfield, one of the main chroniclers of 1916, notes:

> [de Valera's] failure to relieve the hard-pressed garrison's position at the Bridge remains one of the most extraordinary aspects of the battle of Mount Street. Seventeen men had kept a whole English battalion at bay for almost five hours of bloody fighting, yet de Valera never made any serious attempt to help them.

By contrast, from their position inside the distant Jacob's biscuit factory, fellow Rising leaders Thomas Mac Donagh and John MacBride made attempts to help the beleaguered Mount Street men. Vinny Byrne – later a leader of the Apostles – fifty years later was able to recall the precise route which he mapped out for MacBride and Mac Donagh: Byrne was little more than a boy at the time, but the two men saw that he had a precise knowledge of practically every street in Dublin – a knack later shared by all the Apostles – and so they asked him for precise directions to Mount Street. Byrne rattled off:

'Cuffe Street, Stephen's Green, Leeson Street, Wilton Place, into Baggot Street, along by the canal to Mount Street and turn into Upper Mount Street. There was a laneway running behind these houses; you could get into the houses and cross over Mount Street to the back of Clanwilliam House.'

Mac Donagh and MacBride decided that Byrne himself was too young to send: but they did despatch a party from Jacob's – and one man was wounded in an unsuccessful attempt to reach Mount Street. Jacob's factory was several miles from Mount Street, whereas de Valera's command post in Boland's Mill was considerably less than one mile away – and between it and the fighting, moreover, there lay leafy gardens which would have provided ample cover for young active men eager to go to the help of their comrades. If we bear in mind such facts, de Valera's decisions become even more incomprehensible.

The result of the executions was to bring public opinion – initially opposed to the Rising, and appalled at the civilian deaths and material destruction that had accompanied it – over to the rebel side. This switch in sympathies would be capitalised upon by Collins and others in the months and years that followed. First one Catholic and Nationalist leader spoke out against British actions, and then another and another, until a tumult of criticism was directed against British policy. The most notable of these voices, and certainly the most unexpected, was Bishop Edwin O'Dwyer, who had hitherto been seen as strongly anti-Nationalist. When the British commander General John Maxwell wrote urging O'Dwyer to curb the rhetoric of two of his outspoken Nationalist-minded priests, the bishop replied by sending him an open letter condemning his lack of mercy towards the prisoners. The IRB had the prelate's letter swiftly reprinted and it was hung in windows throughout the country, neatly framed in tricolour ribbons. The bishop was truly an accurate barometer of the change coming over Irish public opinion. By the time Maxwell was scapegoated and removed from his Irish post in October, he had come to two correct conclusions. One was that the public had come to believe that in one week more had been achieved by the insurgency than by all of Redmond's patient efforts at Westminster. The second was that the root cause of the Rising was the startling tolerance that had been shown to the unruly Orange element in Irish affairs.

But this remarkable change in public opinion appeared to be as remote as space travel when Collins and the other surviving prisoners were first led off to the ships taking them from the docks of Dublin to British prisons. In some instances, indeed, the prisoners had to be protected by soldiers from the wrath of Irish 'separation women', who were receiving allowances because their husbands were absent fighting in the Great War. But even at this moment, even as the prisoners were marched to the boats, there was the occasional cheer and shout of 'Up the Republic!' Liam Tobin, who would in due course become Collins's principal assistant in finding targets for the Twelve Apostles, would later describe a man breaking through the military escort to hurl bars of chocolate in the direction of the prisoners. It was a sign of things to come.

CHAPTER TWO

A Boiling Pot

Crowds in Dublin welcome released Republican prisoners, 1917.

AFTER A SPELL IN VARIOUS BRITISH PRISONS, MICHAEL Collins and most of the other 1916 prisoners were gathered together at Frongoch camp in North Wales. Here, as is customary with Republican prisoners, the internment centre morphed rapidly into a university of sorts, with lessons in history and Republican philosophy the norm. In the heady mix of agitation and political indoctrination which are a continuing characteristic of Irish political prisoners, Michael Collins began noting names and reorganising the IRB. Frongoch acted, in other words, as a remarkable revolutionary springboard, with the prisoners schooled in every known form of propaganda activity. In Ireland, meanwhile, the British began referring to the Rising as a 'Sinn Féin' rebellion – when in fact, this movement, which had been established some ten years previously by the journalist Arthur Griffith, was small and lacking in any degree of influence at the time of the Rising. Indeed, the party had nothing to do with the Rising – and a good deal of Arthur Griffith's political philosophy would have stuck in the throats of the ardent young men and women who joined the Sinn Féin clubs that began to spring up all over the country.

Griffith preached self-sufficiency and a withdrawal from the British Parliament – which was in itself well and good.

However, he also advocated the retention of the monarch for the purposes of the new parliament, so that the rule of law would be in the name of the Kings, Lords and Commons of both Ireland and England. This monarchical cloak-spreading was based on Griffith's observations of the Dual Monarchy of Austria and Hungary, which had been inaugurated in 1867: its function was to keep together these quarrelling halves of the Austrian Empire; and Griffith had written a text, *The Resurrection of Hungary*, which turned on the possibilities this arrangement afforded to the relationship between Britain and Ireland. The book featured in the reading of figures as disparate as General Maxwell, who thought that it contained the seeds of the rebellion, and Michael Collins himself, who had for years studied Griffith's writings with dedication and admiration. This suddenly quaint form of thinking, however, was now swept away – British policies ensuring that a new Nationalist movement sweeping Ireland had a name and a renewed identity; and ensuring too that a revivified Sinn Féin would become the chief political beneficiary of this new political world.

Ireland (and most importantly Irish America, the political clout and influence of which neither side could possibly ignore) now increasingly focused its gaze on Frongoch. It became a place of more potency than the House of Commons – where the sands of time were running out for Redmond and the Irish Parliamentary Party. Though the public did not, perhaps, yet realise it, rapid political and cultural developments were already underway. As the changing political temperature of Ireland became apparent, the British authorities began to seek to assuage public opinion, particularly American public opinion (for the British urgently needed the assistance of the United States in the war against Germany) by releasing batches of prisoners and sending them back to Ireland. Collins himself emerged from Frongoch at Christmas 1916 with a notebook filled with the names of men who would be the warriors of the future. Back in Dublin, he donned the mantle of Thomas Clarke – and that mantle was bestowed upon him by a remarkable woman whose position in Irish revolutionary history has not often been recognised.

This was Kathleen Clarke, Thomas Clarke's widow. I conducted an interview with her on the fiftieth anniversary of the Rising – and now that another fifty years have passed, I believe it should be published again. Kathleen Clarke was seventy-two years old in 1966: her eyes were like large faded sapphires and it was hard to look straight at them without flinching. She herself never flinched: indeed, there is no record of her having ever flinched from anything, even from her memories of the eve of her husband's execution. She told me:

> I thought that in the morning we were likely to be brought before the commanding officer, so I had taken off my blouse and skirt and hung them up, so that I wouldn't look too bad. There were six of us, and we had only one blanket over us. We had been very annoyed at some young British soldiers coming to flirt with us, it was outrageous. Then an officer came and said I had permission to see my husband.

47

'My God, Kathleen,' said one of the girls, 'what does that mean?' 'It means death,' I said. 'Oh no,' said the girl; Marie Perolz was her name. 'Look,' said I, 'do you think that if the British government were going to send my husband on a journey any shorter than to the next world, that they would get an officer and a car out at midnight to go for me?' 'You're a stone,' said the girl. I was.

We were stopped several times. There were snipers on a lot of rooftops and I didn't think we would be let go on. But the officer showed his pass and we got through. Kilmainham [Gaol] was terrible. The conditions! There was a monk downstairs. He told me that my husband had put him out of the cell. There was no light in it only a candle that a soldier held. 'Why did you surrender?' I asked Tom. 'I thought you were going to hold out for six months.' 'I wanted to, but the vote went against me,' he said. We talked about the future the whole time; I never saw him so buoyed up. He said that the first blow had been struck, and that Ireland would get her freedom but would have to go through hell first.

I didn't cry. He had to face the ordeal by himself in the morning. If I broke down, it might have broken him down. I said, 'What did you do to that priest down there?' 'That damned fellow came in here,' he said, 'and told me he would give me Confession if I would admit that I was wrong and that I was sorry. I'm not sorry. I told him that I gloried in what I had done.' I was expecting a baby but didn't tell him that in case it might upset him.

I asked an officer to have his body sent to me. He hemmed and hawed and said he'd had no instructions about it. In the end he promised to do something. But they wrote to me afterwards that I could not have the body for burial. I walked home by myself from the Castle to Fairview. There was a smell of burning in the air. I had to walk in the middle of the road because things were falling off the roofs. In O'Connell Street a big policeman stopped me. When I told him who I was and where I was going, he said, 'You'd better go down Fairview, Ma'am. There are some soldiers up at Parnell's Monument and they are not very nice.' I had to climb over a big pile of rubble in North Earl Street. The bricks were still hot. I never met a sinner all the way home.

I had sent the children down to Limerick and there was no one on the house. I don't drink, but I had whiskey and brandy in the house in case any wounded were brought in. 'Now,' I thought, 'I'll have one twenty-four hours of oblivion'; and I took out a bottle of port and filled myself out a glass, I thought it would be strong. But I was awake again in an hour.

My sister came up from the country and that night a lorry came and took us to Kilmainham to say goodbye to my brother [Ned Daly]. I heard it coming before any of them and I said, 'It's coming to take us to Ned. He is going to be shot.' They thought I was going off my head. But a few minutes later, we all heard it. Then it stopped outside the house. My sister didn't want me to go but I insisted. My brother was in uniform. He looked about eighteen. There was a group of officers outside the cell, they seemed to have some spite against him. The soldier holding the candle had been in my husband's firing party. He said my husband was the bravest man he'd seen. I lost the baby a week later. I don't know if it was a boy or a girl. I worked at the prisoners' fund even when I was in bed. It saved me from going mad. God must have put the idea in my head.

For several months after the Rising, Kathleen Clarke was the person who kept the revolutionary flame alive. She was the important contact with such significant Fenian leaders in America as John Devoy, who had helped to finance the Rising. In its aftermath, Devoy directed the considerable funds collected in America to Kathleen Clarke: she ran the National Aid Fund which helped to alleviate the hardship of families and survivors of the rebellion. Such funds, as well as fulfilling a vital need, also provided a bridge from the time of the 1916 surrender to the return of the prisoners, including Michael Collins. Apart from his kindness to her husband, Kathleen Clarke knew Collins's Frongoch reputation as an organiser and conspirator: and after a *pro forma* interview, he took over the running of the Fund on 19 February 1917. Like her, he saw the Rising as only the beginning. The real war was yet to come.

Michael Collins was now at the helm of a new ferment in Ireland. This organisation and direction of the new Sinn Féin, however, was by no means all plain sailing: indeed, a period of internal politicking took place involving Sinn Féin and the wider Irish Volunteers, with the aim of shifting attitudes, changing hearts and minds, and persuading public opinion that violence was sometimes both necessary and desirable in order to further Nationalist ends. Collins – focused now on building up a political as well as a military machine – approached the task cautiously. It was no mean feat to bring about such a shift in the public mood: to condition large masses of people to the prospect of future violence, and to steel them for the task and for the suffering that would undoubtedly flow as a result; and certainly it was the case that neither the public at large nor the youthful ranks of the Volunteers in particular could be presumed to be naturally disposed to drastic ways and means. In a memorable passage in *Remembering Sion*, Pearse's literary executor Desmond Ryan describes the reaction of the first Volunteer to kill a policeman after the Rising. He struck the officer with a hurling stick during an anti-Conscription rally – and Ryan wrote:

> There is madness in his eyes. He sees Mills again and again with his bloodstained head and his eyes haunt him. He groans and moans and relives the scene. [...] He falls asleep. [...] For a week, O'Dwyer is restless and haunted. In his dreams he moans and mutters. At last Mick [Collins] sends a sailor man and with eyes still horror-shaded, O'Dwyer vanishes to America.

Pearse's mother Margaret first gave the stricken Volunteer a room in Cullenswood House, the family home. But she disapproved of what he had done. As far as she was concerned, 'war was one thing, murder another'.

These were stirring times. The period between Christmas 1916 (when Collins was released from Frongoch and returned to Ireland) and 1919 (when Collins formed the Squad, the team of hitmen destined to become known as the Twelve Apostles) saw not only the ever-growing strength of the Volunteers and of Nationalist sentiment generally, but also the slow but inexorable destruction of the Irish Parliamentary Party and the ending of John Redmond's political career. It also witnessed a growing – though not overtly acknowledged acceptance – of the idea of Partition, as well as the beginnings of strain within the ostensibly unified Sinn Féin movement – strain that would in time prove to have the gravest possible repercussions. History remembers this strain as manifesting itself principally in the tense relationship that developed in this period between Collins and Éamon de Valera, later his principal rival for the leadership of Irish Nationalism. I will examine this rivalry later – but for now, it is important to note that the Collins–de Valera duopoly was not the only significant factor at play at this time.

For this era was one of growing influence for the founder of Sinn Féin, Arthur Griffith – a development that simply could not have been foreseen in the period before the Easter Rising. Griffith, as we have seen, had taken no part at all in the Rising itself: he was essentially constitutional in his aims and methods, and this was a point he himself had made again and again, in article after article for his newspaper the *United Irishman*, for more than a decade. Collins had been an eager devourer of the newspaper since boyhood, and in the aftermath of the Rising he continued to admire Griffith – even if the older man's notion of a Dual Monarchy of Britain and Ireland now began to seem undesirable to more and more people.

Griffith remained, however, the notional leader of the Sinn Féin movement that he had founded; and Sinn Féin remained the label attached to the new movement sweeping Ireland. The pragmatic Collins understood perfectly well, therefore, that he would do well to learn to work with Griffith, and in particular to come to an arrangement with him on the matter of violence versus constitutional politics. It was a tense time: for the simple fact was that Griffith did not think that the country was ready for warfare, either militarily or psychologically. Collins, on the other hand, was convinced that the best course for the nation was a continuation of what had begun in Easter Week 1916: and so he continued his infiltration of Sinn Féin, assiduously placing his men and women where he could within the organisation. Collins and Griffith *would* learn, as we will see, to work together: indeed, they had no option but to do so, as the world changed and changed again before their eyes.

For wider Irish Nationalist opinion, the most immediate pressing task was to prevent the imposition of Conscription – frequently threatened but still not applied by the British – across Ireland. For the British, the extraordinary loss of life on the Western Front meant that a new source of manpower was becoming a more and more pressing issue – but naturally Irish Nationalism did not see it in quite the same way. The Irish landscape rang with the sounds of sedition, as public meeting after public meeting attracted vast crowds determined to rally against what they correctly saw as a threat to the lives of Ireland's young men.

The British authorities had a relatively potent weapon to hand as a means of countering the growing disorder: the Defence of the Realm Act (originally passed in 1914 at the outbreak of war) enabled special measures to be taken by the security forces as necessary – and now the Royal Irish Constabulary (RIC) took to breaking up anti-Conscription meetings through an enthusiastic deployment of the baton, that indispensable tool of Irish political activity. The 'seditious activity' proscribed by law came to be used to describe all manner of activities, from the singing of rebel songs to drilling with 'Tipperary Rifles' (hurling sticks); and courtrooms filled up with improbably youthful defendants – such as the lad who was accused of looking at a policeman 'in a humbugging sort of way'.

In London, Herbert Asquith's administration fell from power at the end of 1916, the Liberal Party split once more, and David Lloyd George took over at the head of a coalition of Liberals and Conservatives. Edward Carson now joined the cabinet – and Lloyd George set about drawing up new Home Rule proposals to replace the provisions passed by the Commons in 1914, but frozen for the duration of the First World War. One result of Lloyd George's new formula would be the political death of the once powerful Irish Parliamentary Party, and the fall from power of Redmond.

In February 1917, George Plunkett, Papal knight and father of the executed Joseph Plunkett, won a parliamentary by-election for Sinn Féin in County Roscommon, vanquishing in the process the Parliamentary Party candidate. It was a sign of things to come. Another vacancy occurred in neighbouring County Longford a short time afterwards: and Collins selected as the Sinn Féin candidate one of their comrades in jail, the still-interned Joseph McGuinness. His election poster was surely one of the most famous in Irish election history: it showed a man in convict uniform with the slogan 'Put him in to get him out' – and the poster proved to be a palpable hit, for the electors of Longford *did* put him in. This was a yet more serious blow to the Irish Parliamentary Party, who in different and less politically fraught circumstances might have counted on winning such a seat in their electoral heartland. Plunkett had won *his* seat on an understandable sympathy vote laced with a strong dose of Nationalist feeling. But in Longford, here was a prisoner in jail standing for election and winning – and in the process convincingly demonstrating the growth of Sinn Féin and the dramatic and seemingly inexorable eclipse of the Parliamentary Party.

The Longford by-election, however, was significant in other ways too: for it marked the first serious disagreement between de Valera and Collins. As the by-election approached, the former had written from jail in Britain warning that the nomination of a Sinn Féin candidate was, at this point, a step too far, and could lead to trouble. But now other by-elections began falling Sinn Féin's way; and at the same time Lloyd George decided to release all the prisoners still held in British jails. De Valera now managed to swallow his objections to by-elections: indeed, in July 1917, less than a week after his release, he was actively campaigning for himself in a by-election in County Clare. He won, and again, the Parliamentary Party candidate was defeated with ease.

Collins was ever more emboldened. His vision was based on a premise of pursuing electoral advantage, while simultaneously moulding his young followers into hardened Volunteers prepared to follow the path of active service in order to gain their ends – and there was every indication that this radical path was the correct one. The idea of force – distasteful as it was to the likes of Griffith – was now moving into the Republican mainstream. But de Valera was not convinced: his own experience of fighting had left him unwilling to lightly follow the path of physical force. Now he began – in a foreshadowing of later splits in the Republican movement – to gather like-minded followers, among them Cathal Brugha and Austin Stack, two of the most prominent critics of Collins and his ways.

Indeed, during this period, and as events continued to spiral towards what now began to seem to be inevitable warfare, it is clear with the benefit of hindsight that Collins was obliged to expend as much energy on combatting oppositional forces within the Volunteers and the wider Sinn Féin movement as on strategising against British rule in Ireland. It is crucial to underscore this point, for it emphasises the breadth of opinion within an ostensibly united Republican front. Collins, however, remained convinced that, ultimately, the parliamentary route was nothing more than a useful side-strategy; and that warfare alone would serve their ultimate ends. And so he pressed on.

As the Volunteers engaged in illegal military drilling, and as full-blooded treasonable oration was delivered from Sinn Féin platforms up and down the country, so counter-arrests mounted up. A key plank in Collins's policies was that of civil disobedience – in this case, by a rapidly spreading public refusal to recognise the legitimacy of the courts established to try those arrested for seditious activity. Public opinion increasingly favoured and cooperated with such methods – and as time passed, so Collins appeared more and more justified in his policies. Sometimes, he seized the opportunity to outline such views, in electrifying and theatrical terms. One such occasion took place in September 1917, over the grave of Thomas Ashe, who had taken part in one of the few successful operations of 1916: an ambush of police in Ashbourne in County Meath. In custody, Ashe decided to go on hunger strike and was force-fed: this clumsy – not to say brutal – process killed him, and his funeral was a vast occasion marked by volleys fired over his grave. As the echoes of the shots died away, Collins stepped forward and delivered a short, powerful message in Irish and English:

> Nothing additional remains to be said. That volley which we have just heard is the only speech which it is proper to make above the grave of a dead Fenian.

Other elements in this political drama also continued to work in Collins's interests. In particular, the British government now played into his hands – and overplayed its own – concerning the fraught issue of Conscription, which at last came to a head.

Sustained German military pressure in this final phase of an exhausting world war caused Field Marshal Henry Wilson – himself an Irishman, and a close advisor of Lloyd George – to redouble his efforts to get his hands on Irish manpower. The British cabinet was now informed that with Europe 'in anguish', Ireland had 'no real grievances'; but that in spite of this state of affairs, the country was in a state of rebellion. The presence in the cabinet of such committed Unionists as Bonar Law, Carson and Foreign Secretary Arthur Balfour ensured a sympathetic reception for such observations.

However, nobody mentioned the stark fact that out of one hundred and seventy thousand Irish Volunteers on the eve of the First World War, almost ninety per cent had answered Redmond's urgings to join up – and that tens of thousands of these had died fighting for the king. Wilson was rather more concerned with other facts: especially with the knowledge that in France, the British army was now under severe pressure along a fifty-mile stretch of the Western Front; and that there were, by his calculations, one hundred and fifty thousand 'recalcitrant Irishmen' shirking their responsibilities. Conscription, urged Wilson, must now be extended to Ireland – and Lloyd George now accepted his analysis.

In April 1918, therefore, Conscription proposals were brought forward. The Prime Minister sought to sweeten the pill by publishing a report from a convention established in the aftermath of the Rising to establish a plan for the governance of Ireland. Here at last, he was setting out his vision for the pursuance of Home Rule in Ireland – and it was a rather different form of Home Rule from that championed by Redmond and passed by the House of Commons in 1914. The report, which was published in April 1918, contained a version of Home Rule whereby the Westminster Parliament retained very substantial powers: a new Irish parliament was to have no control over the army or navy, or Customs and Excise, or the postal service – all until such time as Westminster was ready to repatriate these powers. Given the pre-war delays and postponement of Home Rule, such new proposals were hardly reassuring to Nationalists – who were also considerably underwhelmed by the fact that forty per cent of the seats in the lower house of the proposed new parliament were to be allotted to Unionists. The country erupted in protest. In Britain, Redmond led the Irish Parliamentary Party out of the House of Commons – never to return. In Ireland, de Valera led a Sinn Féin delegation to Maynooth where the Irish Catholic Hierarchy was holding a meeting: he demanded and received an episcopal letter denouncing Conscription, which was read out from the pulpit of every Catholic church in the country.

Then, a month later, what became known as the 'German Plot' swoops took place. They were triggered after an Irishman, Joseph Dowling, was put ashore on the County Galway coast from a German submarine – and promptly arrested in a pub, his first and only port of call. The exact nature of Dowling's mission was never clarified – though there were indications that Collins had had wind of it – but the episode provided an excellent government pretext to initiate a widespread series of arrests. Amongst those incarcerated at this time were both

Griffith and de Valera: Collins's efficient intelligence network had tipped him off that the arrests were in the offing, and he had ample time to warn those on the list. In the event, however, the Sinn Féin leadership decided that there were propaganda points to be earned from further periods of incarceration in British jails: and those on the list remained in their homes, and were duly arrested and shipped across the Irish Sea.

The effect of this wave of arrests, however, was felt in ways that not even Michael Collins could have predicted. De Valera already had a certain prestige in the public mind as the only battalion commander to survive the Rising – and now his arrest added further to his power and authority, and diminished the standing of Collins, whose IRB allies suffered setbacks in elections to the Sinn Féin and Volunteer executives. De Valera was able to further enhance his authority by persuading Griffith to stand down in his favour as President of Sinn Féin; later, de Valera also became leader of the Volunteers. Collins, of course, remained as skilful and canny as ever: he lost no time, for example, in setting out to infiltrate and organise every faction and grouping he could identify in the ever-changing Republican movement. The point also needs be made that, from June or July 1919, Collins was head of the Supreme Council of the IRB, which position in the eyes of that organisation made him de facto leader of the country.

At the end of that year, the conclusion of the First World War brought a general election – and the panel of Sinn Féin candidates drawn up by Collins and his close friend and collaborator Harry Boland swept the board. As Frank O'Connor noted later, in the selection of this panel moderation was not allowed to show its 'hideous fangs'. As we shall see, this particular piece of skullduggery would return to haunt Collins later.

But the immediate objective was achieved. The Irish Parliamentary Party was shattered, winning only six seats to Sinn Féin's seventy-three; with the Unionists taking the remaining twenty-two Irish constituencies, mainly in the north-east of the country. Sinn Féin candidates had stood on a platform of Republicanism and abstention from the British parliament – and now they were as good as their word. On 21 January 1919, this abstentionist parliament – or Dáil, as it was known – met for the first time in the Mansion House in central Dublin. Cathal Brugha read out the Democratic Programme, based on the 1916 Proclamation, which it was intended this Dáil would pursue. There were no Unionists present; and now the reality of a looming Partition of Ireland could no longer be ignored. The significance of the day – with its sense of a rapidly changing world – was further underscored by events taking place at Soloheadbeg in the west of County Tipperary, even as the Dáil was in session. Soloheadbeg is remembered in Irish history as the scene of the first deliberate killing of state security agents by Republican agents: here, in an unsanctioned initiative, a party of Volunteers led by Seamus Robinson, Dan Breen and Seán Treacy deliberately shot dead two members of the RIC who were transporting a cartload of gelignite for use at a local quarry.

Collins was one of the few leading Republicans to welcome the killings. For most observers, however, this was a troubling development: the dead RIC men were, after all, Irishmen and family men; when they were shot, moreover, their rifles were slung over their shoulders, meaning that they were essentially unarmed; they might instead have simply been held up, relieved of their gelignite, and sent on their way. The killings, then, sparked tension in Republican ranks – but they were significant in other ways too: from this moment, Republican operatives began to be referred to not as Irish Volunteers, but as members of the Irish Republican Army – the IRA, an acronym which now passed into common usage. The French historian Yves-Marie Goblet caught the mood of the moment most accurately, remarking in *L'Irlande dans la crise universelle, 1914–1920* (1921) that 'a new epoch was beginning and one that would be terrible'. Indeed, as 1919 wore on, more and more people on the Nationalist side came to accept the argument that the Dáil, which had after all been elected by the democratic vote of the people, had declared a Republic – and that this Republic had the right to defend itself by use of force against those who would attack it or its agents.

Collins himself was not present at the meeting of the first Dáil at the Mansion House. He and his friend Harry Boland were in Britain conducting a successful attempt to spring de Valera from Lincoln Jail, where he had been held since the German Plot swoops. Jailbreaks, indeed, would form an essential part of the Sinn Féin and Republican story – though it is safe to say this one was one of the most audacious of all. De Valera had previously managed to smuggle out the impression of a key to the prison gates on the soft wax of a candle he had purloined while attending Mass: and this had been carefully copied onto a postcard illustrated with a large key and a prisoner exclaiming that he couldn't get in or get out. It had taken a little time for the meaning of such a message to sink in: but on the night of 21 January, Collins and Boland were standing outside the prison gates. Collins now tried his facsimile key – which broke in the lock; but de Valera was nevertheless able to push out of the lock the broken portion of the key, and then successfully turn the lock. De Valera went to ground in various Manchester safe houses, while Collins returned to Ireland.

De Valera himself took his time about returning to Dublin. Indeed, he caused consternation amongst his colleagues by announcing that he intended to go, not to Dublin at all – but rather to New York, where he felt he could do more to highlight the Irish cause. His followers feared that such a speedy departure would nullify the effects of the publicity bonanza achieved through his escape, by giving the impression that de Valera was skipping the country simply to get away from the trouble that was clearly building up at home. With this in mind, Cathal Brugha was despatched to Britain to persuade de Valera to return to Dublin. This he eventually did, though on a temporary basis only: for in June 1919, Collins arranged for de Valera to be smuggled out of the country, bound at last for the United States. A new phase in the struggle was now underway.

CHAPTER THREE

Enter the Twelve Apostles

Collins's men: Apostles Jim Slattery and Joe Dolan are seated second and third from the left, and William Stapleton second from the right. Dublin Brigade members Joe Leonard and Charlie Dalton are seated, respectively, far left and far right, while the standing figure, clutching a white hat, is Adjutant General Gearóid O'Sullivan.

WITH THE DEPARTURE FOR THE UNITED STATES OF DE Valera, Michael Collins gained a freer hand on the domestic front. Arthur Griffith had been appointed acting President of Sinn Féin – but Collins was actually in control, and his influence was felt more and more throughout the entire Republican network. Collins actually held four formal posts: those of Adjutant General, Director of Organisation, Minister of Finance – and Director of Intelligence, the position that of course bears most directly on the subject of this book. He was therefore obliged to be – and he was – exceptionally well organised, managing to keep all his multifarious activities in watertight compartments and fully screened one from the other. Indeed, Collins's discretion in his intelligence activities was such that his operatives, even those working together inside, for example, the corridors of Dublin Castle, had to be introduced to each other as secret colleagues and fellow conspirators.

This genius in the arts of compartmentalisation served Michael Collins well – operationally speaking. It did, however, have one unfortunate side-effect – and this was to foster bitterness and resentment among some of his fellow Republican leaders. The first Dáil had appointed Austin Stack Minister of Home Affairs, with a brief to establish a new national civil service and courts system to rival and, it was envisaged, eventually replace the British systems operating in Ireland. However, though a courageous man and a celebrated Kerry footballer, Stack was not noted for efficiency. He had been in charge of the arrangements both to get Casement to safety after he landed in Kerry prior to the 1916 Rising, and for the safe landing of a shipment of 20,000 German rifles around the same time. But both operations were spectacularly bungled: the captain of the arms ship, for example, was ultimately forced to scuttle his vessel when a British ship came into view; he had never received the expected signal. Collins incurred Stack's enmity when in front of colleagues, he told Stack that his management of his department was a 'bloody disgrace' – and so Stack had his reasons to resent and dislike the dynamic Collins. 'I'll get even with you,' he told his colleague – and, as we will see, he did get even.

As Collins's influence grew, meanwhile, Cathal Brugha (who like Stack had never in any case been inclined towards his colleague) also became increasingly jealous. As Minister for Defence, Brugha was nominally Collins's superior. He had his virtues as a commander: he was, for example, extraordinarily courageous. Yet, he had neither Collins's strategic capacity nor his vision. It was nevertheless a combination once encapsulated neatly and cruelly by Richard Mulcahy, the Volunteers' Chief of Staff, who noted that Brugha was as 'brave and as brainless as a bull'. The circumstances of the Rising had left Brugha prone to disenchantment with Collins's IRB: and, like de Valera, he had left that organisation – and now regarded Collins's activities with ever-growing suspicion.

Brugha's antipathy toward the IRB, indeed, gave him a particularly odd attitude toward Collins. Like MacNeill before him, Brugha had envisaged the Volunteers as a purely defensive force: then, as the situation hardened, he swung over to an extreme view; and while Collins was organising his intricate and sophisticated intelligence operations, Brugha was working on a decidedly unsophisticated, not to say outlandish, scheme to assassinate both members of the British cabinet, and hostile newspaper editors. This latter notion, of course, speaks volumes about Brugha's views on the freedom of the press: and had it been (as it were) executed, it would have been calamitous for Sinn Féin, an organisation which was deeply aware of and heavily reliant upon the power of publicity.

Spies and informers, however, were another matter. Later, writing in the *New York American* in 1922, Collins wrote:

England could always reinforce her army. She could replace every soldier that she lost, but there are others indispensable for her purposes that were not so easily replaced. To paralyse the British machine it was necessary to strike at individuals. Without her spies England was helpless. It was only by means of their accumulative and accumulating knowledge that the British machine could operate. Without the police throughout the country, how could they find the 'man they wanted'? Without their criminal agents in the capital, how could they carry out the 'removal' of the leaders that they considered essential for their victory? Spies are not so ready to step into the shoes of the departed confederates, as are soldiers to fill up the front line in honourable battle. And, even when the new spy stepped into the shoes of the old one, he could not step into the old man's knowledge.

A *de facto* intelligence headquarters was now established in Dublin's north inner city: as a result of a chance meeting with the hypnotising Collins, the publican Liam Devlin – who ran his eponymous public house on Parnell Street – gave the use of his establishment to his new friend. A core group met nightly at Devlin's, consisting of Collins himself, Gearóid O'Sullivan, Liam Tobin, Diarmuid O'Hegarty, Piaras Béaslaí, Frank Thornton, Tom Cullen and Joe O'Reilly. In the homely Devlin's setting, plans were laid, the events of the day were assessed and out-of-town Volunteer leaders were given orientation lessons. These men, in addition, seldom left Devlin's without a hearty meal provided by Mrs Devlin; and curfew restrictions meant that such visitors were often given a bed for the night. This pub in the heart of Dublin was a truly invaluable meeting place: and in addition, the fact that patrons were coming and going all day provided an additional – and invaluable – cover for Collins and his men.

As Director of Intelligence, Collins had turned to four men in particular to head his intelligence operations. One was Liam Tobin, another 1916 veteran – and like Collins, a Corkman. The second and third were Tom Cullen and Frank Thornton, also Frongoch graduates who took part in a side-activity – selling life insurance – that was an ironic choice of career for men involved in the taking of life. This work, of course, served as a useful cover – but it was rather more than simply this, for the New Ireland Assurance Company was indeed a *bona fide* operation which the ex-prisoners set up with a view to keeping insurance revenues in Ireland. The fourth man was Joe O'Reilly: and he was one of the most sympathetic figures involved in Collins's manifold operations. O'Reilly was yet another Corkman and Frongoch graduate with so many roles that his position was difficult to describe. He was both Collins's 'go for' and 'go to' man' – and he did everything for his boss. Collins was in the habit of visiting each of his scattered intelligence centres: he cycled around Dublin talking his way through roadblocks and relying on his wits, a good suit, and the force-field of his personality to navigate manifold tricky situations. He relied too on O'Reilly to get him anything he wanted, to arrange meetings and to act as a sort of emotional punchbag whenever his nerves or strain got the better of him. Frank O'Connor probably came nearest to summing up the relationship between the two men when, after describing his multiple duties, he described the long-suffering O'Reilly's role as being like that of a 'medieval page'.

The team built up under Tobin, Thornton and Cullen retained a remarkable solidity and consistency in the course of those violent years. The names read like a litany of mutual friendship: Mick McDonnell, Vinny Byrne, Frank Saurin, Joe Dolan, Joe Guilfoyle, Charlie Dalton, Paddy Caldwell, Dan McDonnell, Peter McGee, Paddy Kennedy, Ned Kelleher, Jimmy Conroy and Joe Leonard. This brotherhood, then, was certainly not a fixed team of a dozen members, as the 'Twelve Apostles' nickname would suggest. It was instead a fluid grouping, which was occasionally augmented by members of other IRA units, and which met at Crow Street in central Dublin, a stone's throw from Dublin Castle itself. The unassuming offices at Crow Street would become an extraordinary nerve-centre for Collins's intricate intelligence operation – though this, alone of all his centres and offices, was never visited by the boss himself.

What were these men like? In general, they were pious individuals, whose Christianity was reflexive and could be taken for granted. This piety, however, was readily meshed with the deeds they were called upon to undertake in defence of Ireland – and with the occasional philosophical and doctrinal aid laid on by sympathetic priests, they did not regard the taking of life while under orders as being wrong. After all, they were clear that their cause was just – with this sense of virtue in mind, indeed, the stocks of their rifles were sometimes draped with rosary beads. Seamus Robinson, whose name is associated with Soloheadbeg, was once asked by a woman who knew his record: 'Seamus, how will you go to Confession…?' Robinson's reply encapsulated the attitude of many of these men: 'When I go to Confession,' he told his morally anxious friend, 'I go to confess my sins, not to boast of my virtues.'

Of course, not all of these individuals were slung about with rosaries. Dan Breen, for example, was an almost militant atheist: later, however, he would describe how, during the Civil War, a party of his men were led to 'a very fine statue of the

Blessed Virgin' in the garden of a 'Mr. Fitzgerald' who did not support their anti-Treaty views:

> Taking rosary beads from his pocket he said, 'Boys, this is the fifteenth of August, Lady's Day: kneel down and we will say the Rosary.' The men knelt down and producing their beads, answered very devoutly the decades which were given out by Mr. Fitzgerald. When they were finished they blessed themselves and stood up. 'Now, boys,' said Mr Fitzgerald, 'I'm going to make you a promise. None of you boys here present will be killed in this war.' That promise was upheld.

This reverence for the icons and practices of their religion never deserted the Volunteers – even though by the time of the Blessed Virgin incident, the Catholic Hierarchy had issued a pastoral excommunicating those who found themselves on the 'wrong' Civil War side, and denouncing their activities as murder. Such devout Volunteers fought on regardless. As for Collins himself, throughout the whirlwind of assassinations and killings, he famously remained a Mass-going Catholic.

Most of these incidents, of course, lay in the future: I bring them up at this point only to glance at the character and nature of these individuals now coming together under Collins's banner. I was fortunate enough to interview, many years later, one of the most prominent members of the Squad. This was the legendary Vinnie Byrne: and he impressed me with his intelligence and total recall of the momentous events in which he participated. Accordingly, I reproduce below his invaluable testimony (to the Irish Bureau of Military History) of how Crow Street and the Squad were organised. His account of the formation of the Squad differs from other memoirs, in that he insists that the Squad did not come into operation until March 1920. Such differences of opinion are perhaps inevitable, given the fact that the survivors of those days gave their recollections some thirty years after the events described. For example, Mick McDonnell, who was generally agreed to have been the first leader of the Squad, recounts that its operations began on May Day 1919 – whereas Paddy Daly recalls that *he* was the first leader, not McDonnell! (In addition, he insists on a formation date of 19 September 1919.)

Vinnie Byrne, however, had in his possession a document which states that he left his full-time employment on 9 March 1920, and recounts that the reason for leaving his job was 'the formation of the first whole-time Squad which consisted of twelve men who were also known as the Twelve Apostles'. In his witness statement, Byrne goes into exact detail as to the formation not only of the Squad, but of its ancillary services; he also records the activities and presence of such figures as Dan Breen who sometimes assisted in the Squad's operations.

From the time of the publication of Béaslaí's *Michael Collins and the Making of a New Ireland* in 1926, the names of the Squad members and the intelligence and Dublin Brigade personnel associated with them have been generally available. From cross-checking with other accounts, I suggest Byrne's statement can be regarded as being both authoritative and comprehensive.

SQUAD PERSONNEL

FIRST PART-TIME SQUAD: Mick McDonnell, Tom Keogh, Jimmy Slattery, Paddy Daly, Joe Leonard, Ben Barrett, Vincent Byrne.

FIRST FULL-TIME PAID SQUAD: Mick McDonnell, Tom Keogh, Joe Leonard, Paddy Daly, Ben Barrett, Vincent Byrne, Sean Doyle, Paddy Griffin, Eddie Byrne, Mick Reilly, Jimmy Conroy.

AFTER SOME TIME THE SQUAD WAS STRENGTHENED BY THE FOLLOWING MEMBERS: Ben Byrne, Frank Bolster, Mick Keogh, Mick Kennedy, Bill Stapleton, Sam Robinson. Owen Cullen (Member of 2nd Battalion) was driver for a short time, and Paddy Kelly of Clare for a short time.

INTELLIGENCE STAFF
Director of Intelligence: Michael Collins
Deputy: Liam Tobin
2nd Deputy Director: Tom Cullen
3rd Deputy Director: Frank Thornton

MEMBERS: Joe Dolan, Frank Saurin, Ned Kelleher, Joe Guilfoyle, Paddy Caldwell, Paddy Kennedy, Charlie Dalton, Dan McDonnell, Charlie Byrne.

MUNITIONS STAFF: As far as I can remember, the following were members: Matt Furlong, Seán Sullivan, Gay McGrath, Martin Kelly, Tom Younge, Chris Reilly.

OTHER MEN WHO WERE OUT ON OCCASIONS WITH THE SQUAD:

Dan Breen

Seamus Robinson

Seán Treacy

Seán Hogan

Mick Brennan of Clare

(Robinson, Breen, Treacy and Hogan were members of the Tipperary Flying Squad.)

Byrne summed up for me his memory of his colleagues: 'We were all young, twenty to twenty-four, we didn't think about winning or losing, we just wanted to have a go.' And have a go they did.

Weaponry was, of course, a major problem and one which continued to plague the Volunteers throughout the course of this struggle. Vinnie Byrne has recorded how 'it was the joy of my life when I was handed a .45 revolver and six rounds'. It is interesting to note that a principal supplier of weapons to the IRA – both in Byrne's time and subsequently – was the British Tommy himself. Squad leader Mick McDonnell had a contact in Islandbridge Barracks in Dublin (later renamed Clancy Barracks in honour of a leading Republican who was tortured and killed in Dublin Castle), who supplied purloined arms to the Squad. Another useful source of weaponry was Phil Shanahan's public house in Dublin's Corporation Street, which lay close to one of the capital's flourishing red-light districts. The local prostitutes not infrequently took the opportunity to relieve visiting British servicemen, not merely of their money, but of their weaponry too – and such valuable goods were then efficiently disposed of through Shanahan's. As Dan Breen remembers delicately, 'The lady prostitutes used to pinch the guns [...] at night, and then leave them for us at Phil Shanahan's public house; there was no such thing as payment for these transactions or any information that they gave us.'

McDonnell once dispatched Byrne to another public house – this time on Dublin's Conyngham Road, where two rifles were to be had. The butts of the rifles had been disconnected from the barrels: so Byrne put the butts in his pockets and 'tied the two rifles, one each side of me under my overcoat'. But when he tried to go upstairs on a tram, one of the rifle barrels slipped and fell down the tram steps. Minus the rifles, Byrne was unarmed and he recalled this put him in 'a bit of a fix'. The conductor looked at the rifle barrel and looked at Byrne before commenting, 'That's nice carrying on.' Byrne replied, 'Will you carry on and pick it up for me?' The conductor did so and Byrne 'carried it openly up the stairs'. Subsequently he commented (accurately), 'I was lucky there was no one upstairs on the tram.'

Initially, the Squad kept its arms and equipment at a dump in Mountjoy Court (off Great Charles Street near Mountjoy Square in Dublin's north inner city), on the site of a former stable which was converted into a lock-up garage. The Squad's members would await their instructions just around the corner in St Laurence O'Toole Hall on Seville Place. They were obliged to move to a new location, however, after the British raided Mountjoy Court, and discovered equipment belonging to B Company of the Dublin Brigade. The Squad hastily abandoned the site: the British came back again shortly afterwards, obviously acting under information – but by then the Squad had moved to their new premises in nearby Middle Abbey Street. On the gate of this new building was painted in large letters *Moreland's Cabinet Making and Upholstering*. Byrne describes the premises as being approximately seventy-five feet long – but only twelve feet wide, and flanked on either side by a high wall. The upper floor consisted of two large stores, one of which had a glass roof with an opening window which would have been very useful in the case of a raid (miraculously, none ever materialised). In a second store facing the entrance to the premises, the Squad built a concrete wall four foot high by nine inches thick, to act as a barricade. They also intended to mine the passageway commanded by the wall, but they never got round to doing so.

Nor, needless to say, did they ever get round to doing any cabinet-making. Anyone who knocked at the door of Moreland's seeking a carpenter was met by Byrne, dressed in his overalls, and shaking his head regretfully as he explained that the firm had so much work in hand that they could not take on any more. Byrne was, in fact, a carpenter by trade: and in order to further look the part, he collected a set of tools from Booth's Suppliers on St Stephen's Green. Once he had them safely in his possession, Byrne smoothly handed the unfortunate assistant a note: 'taken in the name of the IRA'. He then constructed a bench and scattered shavings around Moreland's to give the impression of work in progress.

Guns were kept in an old lavatory on the second floor, which in turn was built over another lavatory in the yard below. The door of this room was then bricked up, and the floor of the second-floor lavatory was altered ingeniously so that it could be moved. One of the joists had a six-inch nail driven in, from which hung a mail bag. The guns were placed in this and lowered by rope onto the lower lavatory and were never found: 'it was', Byrne recalled with great satisfaction, 'a perfect job'. The guns used by the Squad were Colt .45 automatics and .45 Webleys; and another founding Squad member, Bernard C. Byrne, describes Tom Keogh, Vinny Byrne and Jimmy Conroy as 'sharp shooters' with the Webley. Bernard Byrne describes the marksmanship of the Squad as being 'particularly high' – this despite the fact that its members never received specialised training.

The Dublin IRA also ran a bomb-making factory which was located in the basement of the Heron and Lawless bicycle shop in Parnell Street in Dublin. This operation began not long after the formation of the Squad – and indeed, there was some overlapping of membership between the 'munitions factory and the Squad'. The bomb-making facility had a remarkably long life for such an institution: it operated for some eighteen months before being raided and replaced elsewhere in the city. The factory manufactured three kinds of hand grenade – known as No 1, No 2, and

No 3, the last being particularly large. The grenades were both percussion and pin models: these initially were not particularly powerful as they were known to explode inside troop lorries without causing any damage. But through trial and error, they gradually became more powerful and more deadly. The trials claimed the life of at least one Volunteer, Matt Furlong, who was killed at Dunboyne in County Meath after the factory had begun to broaden its range and turn out trench mortars and shells.

The single time the Squad received specialist instruction in weaponry came towards the end of the war, when some Thompson guns were smuggled into Ireland, and two former American officers who later joined the Irish National Army conducted some training and demonstration sessions. The Thompsons so fascinated Collins that in one demonstration in which he took part – at the O'Brien Institute in the Marino district of Dublin owned by the Christian Brothers religious order – one of the Brothers dashed out of the building to warn Collins that he was making so much noise that the Tans could be expected any moment.

Collins went to Moreland's at least twice a week. The Squad, who were aware of his enormous workload, greatly appreciated these visits. Vinny Byrne recalls:

The morale effect of his visits was wonderful. He would come in and say: 'Well lads, how are ye getting on?' and pass a joke or two with the rest of us. He was loved and honoured by each and every one of us and his death was felt very keenly by the Squad. I am proud to say that Mick stood by us in our hard times, and that every single member of the Squad stood by him in his hard times, without exceptions.

Byrne's assessment of Collins was shared by the redoubtable Dan Breen, of Soloheadbeg fame. In his memoir, Breen noted that Collins was the one member of GHQ on whom they could all count – and the aftermath of Soloheadbeg itself underscored this fact. This had, after all, always been an unsanctioned operation: and the maverick Tipperary men were generally considered as remaining somewhat outside the pale. Money was tight and they were not paid, relying on the generosity of supporters for sustenance. Breen recalled how, after the Soloheadbeg operation, he had arrived in Dublin expecting to be greeted as a hero – but was met by Collins, who by agreement with the Chief of Staff, Richard Mulcahy, had made arrangements for Breen and his comrades to be spirited to safety in America. Breen, however, made it clear that he was going nowhere, but was instead staying to fight in Ireland. Collins's response was to give a little smile, close his notebook and go about his business, saying only, 'That's fine by me.'

In his particularly useful Bureau of Military History memoir, Frank Thornton makes the point that these men were, or developed into, skilled intelligence operatives – and they required an infrastructure to match. Thornton describes how each geographical area in Ireland came to have its own Intelligence Officer, and this officer assumed the responsibility for establishing a system of information from agents in all walks of life – including the enemy forces. Volunteers were placed within the ranks of the British forces wherever possible and troop movements and the names of spies were recorded. Above the company intelligence officer, meanwhile, was an Intelligence Officer (I.O.) who collated the company information. Information gathered by each I.O. then went to a Brigade I.O. who liaised both with his own subordinates and with IRA GHQ intelligence department.

A chief target for recruitment was an individual who occupied a high position and who was openly supportive of the British. Frank Thornton recalls that it was 'amazing the number of this type of people who, when it was put up to them, eventually agreed to work for us – and did tremendous work afterwards, whilst at the same time keeping the connection with the British forces.' Contacts were made, for example, with political detectives in the G Division – this after Collins himself had spent the night of 7 April 1919 going through secret files held at Brunswick – now Pearse – Street police station, and realised its intelligence potential, an episode we will look at in more detail later. The most notable among these detectives were Edward – Ned – Broy, James McNamara, Joe Kavanagh and David Neligan. All these men had one thing in common – apart, that is, from being detectives. Prior to making direct contact with Collins they had offered their services to Sinn Féin, only to be ignored. Broy, for example, had been supplying information to the O'Hanrahan family (a member of which, Michael O'Hanrahan, had been executed after the 1916 Rising), but initially no one seemed very interested in his information.

Indeed, the others had had similar experiences. Neligan had actually resigned from the RIC and gone home to his native Templeglantine in County Limerick, when Collins contacted him and persuaded him to rejoin as a G-Man. The pair concocted some bogus threatening letters which Neligan was able to show his superiors by way of explanation as to why he wanted to return to his duties. He later went on to become a member of the British Secret Service; he was the spy whose career was sustained the longest. Broy and McNamara both in due course came under suspicion and were sacked; indeed, Broy was actually arrested. However, Collins, by getting another detective to resign, bolstered Broy's plea that someone else could have had access to the typewriter that typed the incriminating notes found in a cache of Collins's seized documents; he then paid this man's passage to America, whence he returned when the war was over. As for McNamara: he came from a Loyalist background – and it was probably his parentage which enabled him to avoid suspicion until almost the end of the war.

Not alone were the detectives able to warn Collins in advance of projected raids: they also supplied their boss with information about who was informing the Castle on Volunteer movements, and what changes in personnel were afoot. In general, then, they opened the book on what had hitherto been a closed and seemingly invincible system. In the early days of the struggle Collins usually met these four at the home of Thomas Gay in Clontarf. Gay was a librarian and his peaceful suburban home was the last place one would have thought of finding high-level assassination planners. The detectives normally travelled to the house by tram, whereas Collins arrived on his ubiquitous bicycle, his normal mode of conveyance for getting around Dublin. As the struggle escalated, however, other secure locations had to be found.

By what Thornton describes as 'all sorts of divers means', contacts were established with 'Army officers, Auxiliary officers and Black and Tans, Sergeants and Privates and before long quite a formidable display of this type of person was on the payroll of our Intelligence department'. One of the most remarkable examples of 'turning' an enemy concerned that of a Major Reynolds who belonged to the much feared 'F' troop unit of the Auxiliaries, a corps whom we will encounter in due course. Remarkably, Reynolds worked hand-in-glove with Crow Street to the very end of the war; and even when he was transferred from Dublin to County Clare, he continued to supply information to Michael Brennan, the Volunteer leader in that county. Reynolds was responsible for passing valuable information about, for example, death squads within the British forces – even to the extent of supplying photographs so that his own colleagues could be followed and shot. Of course, as these contacts' motivation in supplying information was sometimes purely monetary, they were never fully trusted – and in such cases the Collins network would arrange for a second agent to be recruited in each department, with a principal task given to each being the surveillance of the other.

These were skilled operatives – but these individuals were also human, with emotions and vulnerabilities. And the life on which they had embarked inevitably exacted a price. Tobin, for example, was (after Collins himself) the most deadly enemy of the British administration at Dublin Castle. He had a knack for intelligence-gathering that was almost uncanny. He was able to glean, from all manner of unlikely sources, precisely the facts and small details that would lead his associates to their prey – but such work inevitably took its toll, especially as Tobin, and others, were always aware of the circumstances in which the hunters might suddenly become the hunted. Tobin was 'tall, gaunt, cynical, with tragic eyes [...] like a man who had seen the inside of hell. He walked without moving his arms and seemed emptied of energy.'

Collins too was not oblivious to the consequences of his work – suffering from, for example, an onset of 'feeling', of emotion, while he waited in one of his offices for news of a 'job' – a killing – that he had sanctioned. Several contemporary witnesses have spoken of the strange, almost electrical, charge that emanated from him on such occasions. In addition, his daily life was that of a man on the run: escaping from raids, being stopped at road-blocks, sleeping in different houses with no fixed address of his own – and all the while running a war and holding down four different jobs. Somehow Collins managed to survive this frenzied routine, but Tobin was less fortunate, suffering a nervous breakdown in the autumn of 1920. He somehow recovered, however, and was able to resume his career as one of the British administration's most dangerous foes.

Others too were perfectly aware of the price they would be asked to pay, in lives and blood. Broy, for example, advised

Collins that many of the G-Men who would become targets for the Squad were 'decent men': this made it harder to kill them, but kill them they must if success was to be achieved. Neligan too remembers many British servants and operatives as 'good fellows' – but again, he understood and accepted that their lives were forfeit simply by being on the 'wrong' side. This was a deadly game, and these were its rules.

As the struggle intensified on the streets of Ireland, so Dublin began to swarm with 'touts', their business guaranteed by the fact that the 'G-Squad' of intelligence agents depended on each intelligence officer having his own informants. These individuals and their minders tended to meet – as was almost inevitable in so small and intimate a city as Dublin – in the same 'joints', as they were known: establishments such as Kidd's Back public house off Grafton Street, and the Rabbiatti Saloon on Marlborough Street, in the north inner city. The British intelligence officers' concentration on Kidd's Back was understandable given the cardinal rule of intelligence: that operatives have to keep close to the enemy. But it contrasts ludicrously with the lack of resources deployed elsewhere.

One of the British officers, who later received world prominence on account of his talent, was a General Sir Kenneth Strong: he held the rank of Major while in Ireland, and was a brigade intelligence officer stationed in County Offaly. During the Second World War, Strong was appointed Chief of Staff Joint intelligence under General Eisenhower, the commander of Supreme Allied Headquarters. But in Offaly he was given a budget of five pounds a month and told to recruit intelligence sources. He later said of his role: 'I never to my knowledge managed to catch a single Sinn Féiner of any importance. [...] They had been in our net, but because of our ignorance or the unwillingness of witnesses to identify them for fear of reprisals, we had let them go.' When meeting his agents, Strong remarked that 'I would disguise myself as the owner of a donkey cart, but my accent was against me and I had several narrow escapes.' General Strong certainly possessed the English gift for under-statement. The idea of a spy, however brilliant, going about the Irish countryside in a donkey cart, with an upper-class British accent, makes one wonder not how the British lost their Empire, but how they acquired it in the first place. The Strong anecdote goes far to explain how Collins, Tobin, Thornton and the rest of them managed to stay alive during the Anglo-Irish War and how the better-resourced British Secret Service network failed to defeat the Irish effort.

Under such circumstances, relentless and ever-present vigi-lance was a necessity of life. In Kidd's Back one evening, a British intelligence officer rounded on Cullen and exclaimed to the assembly: 'Surely you fellows must know Liam Tobin, Frank Thornton and Tom Cullen? – these are Collins's three officers and if you get those fellows, we should locate Collins himself.' There was no hard evidence that might bring the trio off the streets and into jail – but this was a sudden and salutary reminder that Kidd's Back was not only a pub and intelligence-gathering hot-spot: it was potentially also the ante-chamber to the torture cell in Dublin Castle, which – in the gallows humour adopted by the Squad – was known as the Knocking Shop.

Of course, two could play at that game: for Kidd's Back was also the ante-chamber to the world of the Apostles – and their .45s. One of the dangerous drinking companions cultivated by Tobin was a sergeant in the British army named Fergus Brian Molloy. Molloy was a precious contact, for he worked alongside Colonel Stephen Hill-Dillon, who was the chief intelligence office at Parkgate Street barracks in Dublin – where Lily Mernin, Ireland's Mata Hari, also worked as a secretary for the unsuspecting Hill-Dillon. The relationship between Molloy and Tobin is an interesting one, for it encapsulates the extent to which intrigue and tension filled the atmosphere in the Ireland of the day. Molloy and Tobin circled each other like swordsmen before the fight commences in earnest – not alone at Kidd's Back and Rabbiatti's, but also at another Dublin intelligence rendezvous, Café Cairo on Grafton Street. During their meetings and encounters, an intricate and dangerous game was underway: Tobin trying to get information from Molloy, Molloy trying to ensnare Tobin into embarrassing Sinn Féin by writing down the address of George Plunkett and other notable Nationalist figures on Dáil Éireann notepaper. Indeed, the use of Dáil notepaper to send threatening messages to prominent Republicans was a common tactic at the time – for it enabled the British authorities to claim that the victims had been murdered, in an ostensible sign of Republican splits, by fellow Sinn Féiners. Just how dangerous a game would be evidenced in March 1920 – when Molloy, having become altogether too dangerous a figure in Tobin's intelligence world, was shot dead on Collins's orders. This was a brutal world.

This killing was still to come. The road to Kidd's Back and its dangerous clientele, in fact, may be said to have begun at the end of July 1919, when – as we will see in the next chapter – the Squad officially killed its first G Division intelligence agent on the streets of Dublin. Prior to this, the country had been sliding very obviously into chaos – but both sides were for the moment holding their fire. Lloyd George had warned the new Lord Lieutenant, Field Marshal Sir John French, of the vital importance of placing the responsibility for shedding the first blood on the rebel side. As 1919 wore on, to be sure, French and the Chief Secretary MacPherson grew increasingly restive at this directive – but they were bound to obey orders. It is one of the ironies of Anglo-Irish history that the responsibility for ensuring that such orders were obeyed now fell on those cabinet ministers – Bonar Law and Carson – who had done so much to stoke up tension in the pre-war years. Now they were counselling restraint in Ireland, while work proceeded behind the scenes on formulating some sort of deal that might quell the growing violence while at the same time being acceptable to both Nationalists and Ulster Unionists, as well as to British public and political opinion.

It was an impossible situation – and one of the features of these tension-filled days was that British and Dublin Castle intelligence officials and civil servants began telling their political masters what they thought they would most like to hear: in this case, that the evident tensions within Sinn Féin would inevitably lead to the breakdown of that movement's united front. At the same time, the situation on the ground was so clearly deteriorating that the authorities were driven to 'pro-claim' forms of military rule in various counties across Ireland, proscribing Volunteer activity, banning public gatherings and sporting events – and banning too the increasingly popular Sinn Féin courts that were mushrooming now in many communities.

Ireland, indeed, was increasingly coming to resemble an armed camp. Soldiers patrolled the streets of Dublin with fixed bayonets. A machine-gun post was posted outside Liberty Hall. Various areas of Dublin were cordoned off on a day-to-day basis, and armoured lorries roamed the streets. The *Freeman's Journal* of 12 June 1919 described the Dublin quays 'jammed with tanks, cars, guns, motor lorries and thousands of troops, as if the port was the base of a formidable expeditionary force'. In the London *Daily News*, the seasoned Ireland observer Hugh Martin remarked of the military build-up that:

'government by tanks' is only a temporary expedient and the policy of drift cannot be indefinitely prolonged. There are limits to the most grotesque comedy and in the end we shall have to give up either the hypocrisy of pretending to concern about freedom in Czechoslovakia or the infamy of stamping on freedom in Ireland. The issue may be delayed but it is not in doubt.

But in the event, as we shall see, it was the Irish who fired first.

CHAPTER FOUR

'Stern Necessity'

Seán Hogan's 2nd Flying Column, Third Tipperary Brigade, photographed during the War of Independence.

ALTHOUGH IRISH POLICEMEN HAD BEEN TARGETED IN THE period since the Rising, the first British soldier to be killed met his end at Fermoy in County Cork on 7 September 1919, when the IRA ambushed a troop of the King's Shropshire Light Infantry on its way to church. King George V took this event very personally. He had initially intervened in Irish affairs to comment angrily on the presumption of an Irish-American group of lawyers who, on a tour of Ireland to observe conditions, had become annoyingly vocal at what they witnessed. Now the king wrote to the government demanding that a stop be put to outrageous actions such as had taken place at Fermoy. He wanted to know 'what the Government was going to do to protect the lives of suffering people in Ireland and what measures were to be brought into Parliament for the government of the country?' Acting in response to this unprecedented prompt from the monarch, Bonar Law decided that the only appropriate measure was to suppress the Dáil. The suppression was announced by French the day after the king's letter was received. It was a propaganda coup for Collins.

The Squad might be said to have been *formally* established on 19 September 1919 – even though killings undertaken by men who subsequently were enlisted in the Squad had of course taken place before this date. Collins and Richard Mulcahy, the Volunteers' Chief of Staff, addressed the new unit (at 46 Parnell Square, the headquarters of the Keating Branch of the Gaelic League) on the key elements of their role and methodology. Squad member Paddy Daly later recalled Collins giving:

> a short talk, the gist of which was that any of us who had read Irish history would know that no organisation in the past had an intelligence system through which spies and informers could be dealt with, [and] that now the position was going to be rectified by the formation of an intelligence branch and Active Service Unit or whatever else it is called.

'Whatever else it is called': the name might vary, but the message was clear: the dogs of war had now been loosed. Daly remembered that Collins emphasised that 'under no circumstances whatever were we to take it on ourselves to shoot anybody, even if we knew he was a spy, unless we had to do it in self-defence while on Active Service. He also told us to remember that all members of G Division and the police were not our enemies, and that indiscriminate shooting might result in the death of friends. We discovered afterwards that many of them were our friends.' Collins also warned them that on no account were there to be any private vengeance killings. He later had occasion to haul Daly himself over the coals because he was informed that Daly threatened to kill a detective who had pushed one of his daughters while he was searching the house. Daly was a widower – and he certainly had taken the incident hard. But he assured Collins that he did not and would not harbour thoughts of acting in a purely vengeful fashion – though in view of some inexcusable later behaviour under Daly's command, this protestation has to be taken with a grain of salt. It is the case that overall, the men of the Squad did act in a highly disciplined fashion – although subsequently, the curtain of history was lifted occasionally on some questionable killings.

*

But were they all men? – yes, and no. The assassins who fanned out across Ireland were all men – but many of the critical backroom figures were women – and women loved and trusted by Collins himself. Various histories of this enigmatic man dwell on his love life, of course: this study of the Apostles has no space to dwell on such matters, interesting though they certainly are – but it *is* useful to recall Collins's natural rapport with his women companions, and his ability – not common in a man of his era – to make and keep female friends. And many of these friends were able to assist him, and to play critical roles in this all-encompassing drama.

It is also certain that many of these women associates had been installed by the British in incredibly sensitive roles, and these figures in particular proved to be of incalculable benefit during the Intelligence War. Lily Mernin was one such: indeed, she was one of the most formidable spies of the day. She was a trusted secretary and typist at British military headquarters, frequently typing letters for key figures in military intelligence, and she too took incredible risks, her information forming the basis for many of the Squad's operations. Collins arranged that Mernin be given the keys to a house in Clonliffe Road: this house always seemed to be unoccupied – but it contained a typewriter at which she typed out copies of everything that crossed her desk. She would then leave the house and lock up without ever seeing who came to pick up the dispatches.

As indicated earlier, an extraordinary feature of the intelligence war was the manner in which both sides practically rubbed shoulders with each other during the fighting. Collins took advantage of this circumstance by having Mernin stroll along areas frequented by British agents, such as Grafton Street or Sackville Street, on the arm of such operatives as Tom Cullen or Frank Saurin – and identifying targets for the Squad. It was Mernin who, for example, fingered Molloy for assassination. Molloy, against his own better judgement , had been persuaded to become a spy by none other than Colonel Hill-Dillon, for whom Mernin worked.

Another crucial connection was Susan Mason, a quiet woman who was Collins's intelligence secretary, and who later became an authority on the Irish language. Mason, however, took an oath of silence to Collins, and never broke it. Then there was Collins's own cousin Nancy O'Brien – who one day in the Castle was told that henceforth it would be her duty to handle the most secret coded messages. O'Brien, like Collins himself, had worked in London in the British postal service. When she told her cousin about her new job, the sanitised version of his response went something like: 'How in the name of Jaysus did these people ever get an empire?' O'Brien, showing what must surely have been a family-patented sangfroid, would repair to the ladies' lavatory in the Castle and prepare copies of the secret coded messages for her cousin, smuggling them out of the Castle either in her bra or in a bun drawn up on her hair.

This was nerve-testing work and Collins was not always the most considerate of taskmasters. One day he discovered that a message referring to warders that he had been awaiting had in fact arrived with O'Brien – and she had not recognised its signif-icance. It consisted of a passage of convoluted prose concerning an angel, and light glinting on her hair – all of which O'Brien took to be the imaginings of some love-sick correspondent. 'What sort of an eejit are you?' her cousin inquired with more asperity than tact. O'Brien blew up with wrath, and told him what he could do with his secret messages in future. Later that night, asleep in her house in Howth, she woke up to find Collins standing in the front garden. He told her he wanted to apologise for his thoughtless behaviour, saying, 'I'm under terrible strain.' He then rode off into the night on his bicycle, leaving her a 'little present' on the garden wall – a bag of bullseyes.

Women were often singled out for rough treatment by British-directed undercover units. Women known to be sup-porters of Sinn Féin ran the risk of being raided in their homes by parties of men in plain clothes. These, as Piaras Béaslaí later noted in the first volume of *Michael Collins and the making of a New Ireland* (1926), 'cut their hair and subjected them to other insults and indignities'. Agnes Daly of Limerick, who was a sister of Kathleen Clarke, and a woman known to 'suffer with her nerves', was particularly badly treated in this way: British agents slashed off her hair with a razor – which was also used to inflict a deep wound on her hand.

Eileen McGrane was another significant figure: she was close to Collins, for whom she undertook secretarial duties, and was active in propaganda work for the Republican cause – until she was arrested in her Dawson Street flat for storing illegal intelligence papers. This was a bitter intelligence blow for Collins, and for one of his most valuable informants, Edward Broy, who was arrested because of information gleaned from the McGrane cache. Collins did not rant publicly about Broy's capture, but he was scathing about McGrane's treatment at the hands of what he described as 'English officers and gentlemen'. Even more serious for McGrane, who was a university lecturer, was the fact that she was subsequently court-martialled and sentenced to a jail term in England under harsh conditions. She was the first woman to be court-martialled – though she would not be the last.

In recent years, research undertaken by Meda Ryan revealed another Collins girlfriend who took quite extraordinary risks, and in the process turned the Royal Mail itself into a significant source of information for the IRA. This agent was the improbably named Dilly Dicker. Dicker's grandparents were Sir John and Lady Godfrey who owned a castle in Killarney and additional property in Cork; her father was a senior civil servant. Her home (her parents' guesthouse in Mountjoy Street) was used as a safe house by Collins, who often slept in the attic. Dicker was an accomplished pianist who played the piano at silent movies: she once continued playing as troops conducted an unsuccessful raid on the guesthouse. She was also courageous and quick-thinking: one day she and Collins were walking along Sackville Street (now O'Connell Street) when a hold-up developed in front of them. Collins slipped her his revolver which she thrust into a pocket of her coat only to find, to her horror, that it fell out again just as quickly through a hole in the lining. She bent down, picked it up and, linking arms with Collins, disappeared into a shop – and so avoided the hold-up and being searched.

Dicker carried messages for Collins to the Crow Street team – but her most extraordinary activity lay in mail-sorting. With the help of Collins's agents in the postal service, she would be loaded into one of the large wickerwork baskets that were used to carry mail between Ireland and Britain. Then, concealed beneath a mound of letters, she would be wheeled into the postroom of the mailboat. Here, with the connivance of other workers and dressed in a sorter's uniform, she would take part in the sorting of letters which normally took place on the boat.

In *Michael Collins and the Women in his Life*, Ryan notes that Dicker's activities meant that:

> letters destined for the British Secret Service would find their way into her handbag or her bosom or inside her elastic-legged knickers. She would be met at the other side of the Irish Sea by a man or woman sent by Sam Maguire or Art O'Brien. Letters might sometimes be opened in London but she would usually bring them back to Dublin

to be studied by Mick's [Collins's] sharp eye. On the return journey she would again extract from the mail baskets letters destined for Dublin Castle or for British agents who, Collins knew, were acting as businessmen at addresses throughout Dublin. The names of Mick's suspects became very familiar to Dilly.

As for the women on the other side of the war: it is certainly the case that the IRA did not usually single out women for attack – but there was at least one fatal incident in Cork. This involved a Mrs Lindsay: approximately seventy years of age, and a prominent landowner. She and her chauffeur James Clarke were shot at some point in March of 1921, having been captured in the previous month by Volunteers belonging to the Cork No. 1 Brigade and held as hostages against the lives of a party of Volunteers captured at Dripsey in County Cork as they prepared to ambush British troops. Mrs Lindsay had learned of the ambush in advance, and had informed the authorities accordingly.

Sir Peter Strickland, the British General commanding the area, was a friend of Mrs Lindsay: and following her arrest, she wrote the following imploring letter to her friend:

Dear Sir Peter,

I have just heard that some of the prisoners taken at Dripsey are to be executed tomorrow Monday – and I write to beg that you will use your influence to prevent this taking place and try to reprieve them. I am a prisoner, as I am sure you know, and I have just been told that it will be a very serious matter for me if these men are executed – I have just been told that my life will be forfeited for theirs, as they believe I was the direct cause of their capture. I implore you to spare these men for my sake.

Shortly afterwards, Lindsay followed this letter with another:

Dear Sir Peter,
I am told that 2 more men of the Dripsey Ambush, Dennis Murphy and Barrett, are to be tried tomorrow – will you please for my sake spare these two men. I beg of you to do so, as if these men are spared I shall be allowed to go home, and if not I cannot say what will be my fate.
Yours very truly,
Mrs M Lindsay

Mrs Lindsay never returned home. The six IRA men were executed: the priest who attended them said they were aged between seventeen and twenty-one years of age and went to their deaths like schoolboys. The Cork IRA burned Mrs Lindsay's home, and shot six unarmed teenaged British soldiers and her captured chauffeur in reprisal for the executions.

Mrs Lindsay's sister, Ethel Benson, sought information about her sister's fate some months later. She was replied to by Cathal Brugha, who was Minister for Defence:

In accordance with instructions from the President, I have made inquiries from our local commander in the case of

Mrs Lindsay. The information sent us is that she was executed as a spy some months ago. The charge against her was that she was directly responsible for conveying to the enemy information which led to the execution of five of our men by the British Authorities, to the death of a sixth from wounds received in action, and to a sentence of twenty-five years' penal servitude passed upon a seventh. Mrs Lindsay wrote a letter to General Strickland pointing out the consequence to herself should our men be executed; they were executed nonetheless. Five days after the execution in Cork's barracks, the sentence which had been passed on Mrs Lindsay and suspended pending General Strickland's reply was carried out. We regret the circumstances and the stern necessity to protect our forces which necessitated the action by our local commander.

It must be remarked that this reads like a handwashing epistle, in which the blame for Mrs Lindsay's death is attributed not to GHQ in Dublin but to local action. Whether it was or not is a moot point: senior Republican Oscar Traynor does not make clear whether or not he is referring to the Lindsay case when he talks about the execution of a 'lady' who had given away an ambush. However, he recalls that when the case came before the cabinet (as was always supposed to be the case before executions were carried out), Cathal Brugha objected on the grounds that shooting a woman could lead to the establishment of a precedent whereby the enemy would be better placed than the IRA to find women to execute. In spite of this, however, the unnamed lady that Traynor refers to was executed and he says, 'This was excused, I remember, by a statement to the effect that her execution took place before the notification was received from the Cabinet.'

In fact, what apparently happened was that the commander of the Cork unit from which came the six executed Volunteers took matters into his own hands and ordered Mrs Lindsay's shooting. Quite apart from the actual deaths of the lady and her chauffeur, the incident had an unfortunate sequel. When the Civil War split occurred in the IRA, some of the unit joined the newly formed Garda Síochána, while others took the Republican side. Although GHQ wished to accede to the wishes of the Lindsay family and a number of Protestant clergymen, that the body be disinterred and given Christian burial, the executioners feared that the members of the former Volunteer unit who were now policemen might reveal the whereabouts of the remains – and that prosecutions would follow. The result was that Lindsay's remains and those of her chauffeur were never found.

*

Studying the Apostles in action one inevitably falls to wondering: did they always get the right man? How much real information was there about a target before he was shot? Such doubts are of course the inevitable product of the actions of a ruthlessly efficient unit operating in a war situation in which evidence was assembled not in a courtroom, but rather in other, less legal ways – from scraps of conversation here, for example, or an obscure reference in a letter there, or from an intercepted letter purloined from a sorting office. Such are the rules of an unorthodox war. As for the story of how these individuals kept alive – much less kept functioning as the British reorganised their intelligence services: this is one of the most remarkable tales of warfare anywhere in any sphere. Death was ever present and this stark fact took its toll on friend and foe alike.

The Squad consisted mainly of a core group of working-class men to which as occasion, or targets demanded, other names could be added. As they had to be constantly on standby, and available to be called out on an operation at a moment's notice, Squad members had to be willing to leave their jobs, homes and loved ones in order to go on assignment. In return, they received four pounds, ten shillings a week – a reasonable sum for working men at this time. They were in effect salaried personnel, even if their job description was decidedly unorthodox: they were warned before enlisting not to join if they had scruples about taking human life. Their job, after all, involved assassination pure and simple. Several men who initially signified their willingness to join did indeed cry off when the implications of what was proposed began to sink in. Once the Apostles actually went into operation, however, there is no record of anyone either crying off or betraying their comrades.

The Republican movement had now accepted that the RIC was its natural enemy. Although its rank and file still consisted to a large extent of Catholic Irishmen of the working and small farmers' class, the force operated a skilful intelligence-gathering operation of its own – and now the organisation had to be targeted. De Valera had earlier begun this targeting by unveiling a policy of social ostracism against the RIC: his Dáil statement noted in striking language that:

> The people of Ireland ought not to fraternise as they often do, with the forces who are the main instruments of keeping them in subjection [...] they are spies in our midst. They are England's janissaries [...] they are no ordinary civil force [...] the RIC unlike any other police force in the world is armed with rifle, bayonet and revolver as well as baton [...] the more brutal the commands given them by their superiors, the more they seem to revel in carrying them out against their own flesh and blood [...] These men must not be tolerated socially as if they were clean healthy members of our organised life [...] they must be shown and made to feel how base are the functions they perform...

This verbal assault was stepped up throughout 1919, as unrest spread and clashes between the RIC and Volunteers became more frequent. Intelligence gathered from within the Castle assisted this developing campaign against the RIC, the members of which, it was claimed, were in effect psychologically enslaved and conditioned to serve the British instead of Ireland. As a Castle informant of Collins, one Thomas Markham wrote:

> The RIC had something to do with every phase of government activity. The constable records everything in his diary. What he frightens from the child and coaxes from the cáilín,

what he hears, sees, infers. The sergeant transfers the constable's report, never abbreviating. It is not his part to select. The policeman moves in a social atmosphere, he writes down everything, gossipy servants, what the RIC pensioner says. A 'someone' whose name is never written down. He's a 'reliable source'. He could be the publican. The rail spy, could be the inspector, he frequently is [...] what was said at a Volunteer meeting, where arms were kept...

Ned Broy now came into his own. Hitherto an inconspicuous young police clerk in the British administration, he now morphed into a valued Collins mole – and he sent such reports to his boss, who was now in a position to understand how the system worked. Intelligence gathered by the RIC was transferred to Dublin where it was perused by, interpreted and acted on by the G-Men. People suspected of being disloyal had an 'S' listed after their name; suspects were placed under surveillance in the cities and the RIC barracks in the districts from which they came were notified as to their movements and who they met. Each G-Man had his own notebook, and at night its contents were transcribed to 'a very large book'. Broy's particular value lay in the fact that since 1915 he had been a confidential clerk at G Division headquarters on Great Brunswick Street (now Pearse Street) in Dublin. A copy of every secret report came to Broy's desk, where he worked alone with the 'very large book' in front of him. His insights, in other words, were unrivalled.

Broy also supplied Collins with an invaluable psychological analysis of the RIC – and this showed Collins that a subtle approach could potentially pay large dividends. After all, because of their mainly Catholic backgrounds, and their antipathy towards Freemasonry, many young RIC constables were in fact naturally inclined to be Nationalistic. They discussed Home Rule and other issues quite openly in canteens and other meeting places – even if their rebellious tendencies had been somewhat dampened by the 1916 executions. And so, tutored by Broy, Collins made a point of warning the Squad to be extremely careful about who they shot; some policemen could be friendly, and hence immensely valuable.

Broy's single most important service to Collins took place on the electrifying night I have mentioned previously, 7 April 1919, when he smuggled Collins and an associate, Sean Noonan,* into his room at Brunswick Street police station. Here Collins could literally open 'the very big book', as well as a host of other records. All around him the life of a busy city police station flowed, as he read and transcribed the information, which in effect revealed how Britain held and governed Ireland. It was a remarkable moment.

Many years later I asked Broy, who by then had become Commissioner of the Irish police, An Garda Síochána, why he acted as he did. He told me:

> I come from Kildare. We were reared in a grimmer condition than most. We remembered '98, the yeomanry and what they did. There was a church near where I was born and the Yeos rounded up the women and children, locked them in

---

* Noonan would one day become an Irish Ambassador to Washington and a Director of the *Irish Press* newspaper.

and set fire to the church. We remembered that, the pitch-capping and the flogging and we talked about Wolfe Tone and the Fenians, the Fenians were riddled with informers. After 1916 I felt it was time we learned the lesson.

The lessons were grim indeed: for from the moment he first met Collins, Broy warned him, 'You'll have to shoot.' On 30 July 1919, the Squad did shoot their first intelligence officer: they fired on Patrick Smith, a G Division detective sergeant whose nickname was 'The Dog', and gravely wounded him; he died five weeks later. The targeting of Smith, however, did not happen without an initial degree of hesitation. By chance I came across a man whose father had been sent on Collins's order, to warn Smith that his life was forfeit if he did not immediately leave his G Division duties. Smith was fifty years old and a family man – and he was identified by Collins for several reasons. Chief among these was the vigour with which Smith had prosecuted Béaslaí, at that point the editor of the Irish Volunteers' newspaper *An tÓglác*. Béaslaí had been arrested by Smith, who discovered incriminating documents on his person and duly charged him with making a seditious speech. Collins warned Smith not to produce the documents in court – but he did: and Béaslaí was handed a two-year prison sentence.

All the same, Collins understood the risks of assassinating Smith. In July 1919, he remained intensely conscious of possible negative reactions to the use of force, both within Sinn Féin and Volunteer circles, and among the public at large. He created a firm protocol, therefore: G-Men and other targets were to be warned initially to curb their zeal, and stand down their activities; then, they would be subjected to intimidating treatment, such as being chained to railings, or given verbal warnings. If they heeded these warnings, they would be left untouched – but if not, the Squad would go into operation.

The father of the man I interviewed was a neighbour of Smith. He was thanked for his warning – but told that Smith would not be deterred from doing his duty by any 'young scuts', meaning Collins and Harry Boland. Smith was probably thinking of the occasion on which he had brushed off the representations of Collins concerning the prosecution of Béaslaí – but his decision proved to be a fatal miscalculation – for the Squad now went into action against the obdurate Smith. Mick McDonnell was told to see to it that Smith was killed: and on getting his orders, he selected a hit team to carry out 'the job'. He chose Jim Slattery, Mick Kennedy (who knew Smith by sight), Tom Keogh and Tom Ennis. The men were told to kill Smith when he crossed Drumcondra Bridge in north Dublin on his way home after work. They staked out the bridge for five nights before Smith turned up, but then hesitated to shoot him: Kennedy could not be certain they had the correct target; and Smith further confused the team by taking an unexpected route home. Fearing that their target might have noticed them, the hit was abandoned – and the Squad did not set another ambush for some days.

The end of July arrived – and now they tried again. Smith normally carried a revolver, but did not have it with him on this occasion: and he had no means of defending himself as all four Squad members opened fire on him. They succeeded in hitting him – but, to their astonishment Smith kept running, opened his front door, and fell into the hall. His teenaged son Thomas came to his assistance; and a second son, aged six, pursued his father's assassins, trying – as he explained afterwards – to catch 'those who had shot dada'. Joe Lawless, a Volunteer eyewitness who remained at the scene to check on the outcome of the shooting, records a markedly less sympathetic reaction from an ambulance man who helped to convey Smith to hospital: 'The ambulance man whom I knew as a Volunteer remarked to me, rather disappointedly, I thought, "I don't think he's dead yet."'

Nor was he: Smith, who had been shot four times, lived for some five weeks after the shooting; and McDonnell's verdict was that the Squad 'had made a right mess of the job'. The hit team's worry was that Smith would survive and identify them. But their victim did not identify anyone. He eventually succumbed to the effects of a bullet that had pierced his lung and lodged in his body, but before he died, he made a statement describing what had happened:

When I got off the tram at the end of my own avenue I saw four or five men against the dead wall, and bicycle leaning against the curb stone. Just as I turned the corner into Millmount Avenue, I was shot in the back. I turned and said to them: 'You cowards'. And three of them fired again with revolvers at me. They pursued me to within fifteen yards of my own door and kept firing at me all the time. In all, about ten or twelve shots were fired at me. I called for assistance but no one came to me except my own son.

At the time of the shooting Smith's wife and the remainder of his family had been in the country on holiday; they returned on hearing the news. Smith's sixteen-year-old daughter exclaimed: 'Was it not a cowardly thing to shoot him in the back without giving him a chance to defend himself?' Michael Collins's own analysis of the incident, however, was rather different: his opinion was that the .38 revolvers used by the Squad were the reason that Smith had been able to keep running: and he saw to it that on subsequent 'jobs', the Squad were issued with .45s.

Smith's colleague Daniel Hoey followed him into eternity on 12 September. Again, Collins had his reasons: Hoey was known as a prominent G-Man, active in his pursuit of the Republicans, but his doom was sealed earlier on the day of his death by his contribution to a raid on the Sinn Féin headquarters at Harcourt Street in Dublin. Collins was in an upstairs room when the raid commenced. Below him, the searching detectives found the prominent Sinn Féiner Ernest Blythe and the Sinn Féin Secretary Patrick 'Paudeen' O'Keeffe; and it seemed inevitable that they would get Collins too. Eibhlin Lawless, who was employed in secretarial work in the building, recalled that Collins reacted to the no-warning raid by saying 'We are caught like rats in a trap and there is no escape.' She hid his revolver in her stocking as the raid progressed from floor to floor: and by the time a detective reached Collins's room all incriminating documents had been hidden. When a detective named Neil McFeely entered the room, Collins was sitting on his desk casually swinging his legs. McFeely did not know Collins – but Collins, thanks to Broy, certainly knew McFeely.

Broy had described McFeely to Collins as being 'about the least efficient officer who could be allocated to such work, as he was a man without guile or ruse'. He had only been recently promoted to Inspector, and his police training largely consisted of mapping crime scenes. Broy had further told Collins that McFeely was a convinced advocate of Home Rule, and that the way to unman him was to accuse him of engaging in anti-National activities that would bring disgrace on himself and his family name for generations to come. The stigma of being known as a 'tout' or informer was, after all, traditionally a recipe for ostracism in Ireland. Consequently, when McFeely enquired about some papers his quarry was holding, Collins (according to Lawless) went on the offensive. 'A nice job you've got, spying on your countrymen. What sort of a legacy will you leave to your family, looking for blood money? Could you not find some honest work to do?' The detective recoiled under the onslaught and left the room. Apparently the raiding party had not been told to look for Collins when they searched the Sinn Féin headquarters, for it was assumed that he would never be found in such a public place; and the detectives had therefore been briefed only to look out for lesser figures. Broy later told Collins that McFeely on returning to the Castle told a colleague that he had met a clerk at Harcourt Street, and that he seemed 'a very determined young man'. The detective opined that 'if they're all as extreme as he is, there is plenty of trouble coming'.

Collins, however, understood the danger he had been in: he knew that had it been Hoey rather than McFeely in the room, he would indeed have been 'caught like a rat in a trap'. Hoey was one of the most experienced G-Men: he had been active during Easter week 1916; and had remained active ever since. During a visit to Ireland by American political observers, Hoey had raided the Mansion House while a reception was taking place in the Americans' honour: the plan was to capture Collins – but their prey slipped the net by going to ground in a small dusty room. He emerged when the raid ended, sent his ever-present assistant Joe O'Reilly to get his Volunteer uniform, and re-emerged before the American visitors, resplendent in his new uniform. The visitors were vastly impressed and the Collins legend grew still further. The authorities had taught Collins a lesson, in other words – but Collins was not grateful; and now, in the aftermath of the Harcourt Street raid, he ordered the killing of Hoey.

On the very evening of the Harcourt Street raid, a group led by Mick McDonnell – and again including Slattery and Ennis – waited outside Brunswick Street police station to waylay Hoey, whom they reckoned would come off duty around 10pm. At last they identified Hoey walking down nearby Townsend Street. It had been intended to shoot him at the door of the station – which contained his living quarters – but instead Hoey went into a nearby dairy shop for his nightly glass of milk. Now, McDonnell identified him – and Hoey was shot at the door to the police station garage. This time there was no frantic last-minute dash, for the detective was pronounced dead on arrival at Mercer Street Hospital.

The Apostles had begun their work. I want now to explore in greater detail the codes by which they operated.

CHAPTER FIVE

Apostolic Administrations

The scene of the shooting of magistrate Alan Bell, 26 March 1920. Bell, who was conducting an investigation into Sinn Féin funding, was dragged off a tram in Ballsbridge by 'Apostles' Liam Tobin and Mick McDonnell and summarily despatched.

THE ASSASSINATION TEAMS RUN BY THE SQUAD HAD A particular and highly precise method of identifying, shooting and then finishing off their targets – and it was a method they were obliged, in theory, to follow at all times. The target was spotted and followed; and his identity was confirmed by a member of the Crow Street command who was in theory obliged to accompany each and every Squad 'hit'. The target was then felled with a shot to the head, and finished off while lying on the ground. It was cool, clean, and efficient – or at any rate, so it was described. But it was not always so. The Apostles' third assassination, of Detective Sergeant Thomas Wharton in Dublin on 10 November 1919, was far from clinical.

The principal Squad member on the day was Paddy Daly – and Daly was obliged to locate the target himself. Daly spent some fruitless hours kicking around Harcourt Street (where Wharton was expected to turn up) before he spotted the detective in College Street, near the G Division headquarters at Brunswick Street police station. This was not convenient at all: Daly now had to make his way to Joe Leonard's home in Ranelagh to fetch a gun. On the way back towards College Street – a return journey of four to five miles – Daly, now accompanied by Leonard, chanced to spot Wharton now walking along Cuffe Street with three other detectives. The assassin had been warned by Collins himself that one of these detectives was in fact a double agent and ordered not to shoot him. But this still left Daly and Leonard facing, if not four then certainly three hostile detectives, with only one gun between them. Even so, Daly decided not to waste his opportunity: he fired at Wharton, hitting him once before his gun jammed. The 'friendly' detective joined the other two in drawing his weapon, but did not fire. Instead – and luckily for Daly and Leonard – he stepped pluckily into his companions' line of fire so that they could not shoot – and the two assailants made off safely.

The solo bullet had punctured Wharton's right lung, exited through his chest and then struck a passing girl, wounding her in the head. And there was a further casualty of the whole botched affair: this was James Hurley, a newspaper-seller who had been invalided out of the British Army, having been wounded and gassed in the course of the First World War. Hurley was also in the vicinity of the 'hit' – and William Batchelor, a former British army officer and witness of the scene, claimed that Hurley too had fired on the detectives. For reasons best known to himself, Batchelor testified that he had noticed Hurley hanging about the area for some days before the fatal shooting, and that he had seen him fire 'at two tall men'. In vain did two other newspaper-sellers testify that they had seen Hurley in Little's Bar on the corner of Harcourt Street at the time of the shooting; in vain too did a policeman on point duty testify that Hurley's presence at the scene could legitimately be explained by the fact that he normally sold newspapers there. A British officer's word outweighed that of such witnesses – and Hurley was sentenced to fifteen years in prison.

As bad as this undoubtedly was, it is shocking to realise that, had Wharton been killed in the ambush, Hurley would have been sentenced to death. In the end, however, Wharton survived but was crippled for life; and Hurley, having been released following Irish independence, was shot and killed in the course of the ensuing Civil War as he was helping a wounded man into hospital. The story of the episode is chastening, revealing as it does the undreamed-of collateral perils and dangers that can accompany guerrilla warfare. Batchelor must have been a loquacious gentleman, because in the course of Hurley's trial, he proved to have even more to say for himself. He testified, for example, that he had pursued Daly and Leonard after the shooting. Normally, though not inevitably, passers-by did not interfere with the Squad's activities, although there are reports here and there of outraged citizens courageously giving chase after a shooting – and, probably fortunately for themselves, invariably failing to catch anyone. It may be speculated that Batchelor invented this aspect of his story as he had others. However, it is not speculation to state categorically that the Apostles did not always conform to a doctrine of minimum force. Some of them, Joe Dolan in particular, developed a penchant for emptying the entire contents of their revolvers into their victims' bodies.

*

One of the most amazing features of the entire struggle was the way in which Collins managed to escape identification throughout the period of hostilities. Some of this extraordinary immunity was due simply to his own brazen courage: in, for example, walking up to manned road blocks, engaging in pleasant conversation with those in charge – and then walking off scot-free (and usually with incriminating evidence on his person). For who could connect the pleasant young man in the good business suit with the hulking, thuggish figure of that desperado Michael Collins? Another generally accepted opinion on Collins's continual escapes and seeming immunity from all danger was the fact that the authorities only possessed an outdated and essentially unrecognisable photograph of him. However, I have never been able to understand how this notion fits with the fact that a contemporary publicity film, made on the orders of Collins himself, shows him very clearly, seated at the execution block on which Robert Emmet had been drawn and quartered. With this in mind, I am inclined to think that his immunity was due rather to the fact that he had members of the police force, particularly the Dublin Metropolitan police, so terrorised that when they did see him, they kept quiet about the sighting.

The same questions arise in relation to the Apostles themselves, who were so active and so frequently out on the streets of Dublin that one would have thought that they too would be clearly identifiable as time wore on. There is at least one recorded instance of Squad members waiting on successive occasions to waylay a party of detectives from the Castle as

1. Irish rebels in Stafford jail, 1916, before their transfer to Frongoch. Michael Collins is fifth from the right, marked with a cross.

2. A by-election poster of July 1917 offers the voters of East Clare the choice between the 'felon' de Valera and a repressive John Bull and his Crown Prosecutor.

3. Sinn Féin leaders at a meeting of the first Dáil Éireann, April 1919. De Valera, the Dáil president, is seated in the centre of the front row between Arthur Griffith and Count Plunkett. Michael Collins is seated second from the left, with Cathal Brugha to his left. William T. Cosgrave is second from the right.

4. Harry Boland, Michael Collins and Éamon de Valera in January 1919. The Anglo-Irish Treaty would gravely compromise their friendship.

5. A police notice offering a reward for information on Daniel Breen, whose shooting of two members of the Royal Irish Constabulary (RIC) at Soloheadbeg, Co. Tipperary, in January 1919, accelerated the outbreak of the War of Independence.

6. A group of RIC constables, Castlefogarty House, Co. Tipperary, 1921. Sandbags and barbed-wire defences are clearly visible. Despite the fact that its ranks were filled mainly by Catholic Irishmen, the Republican movement came to view the RIC as its natural enemy.

7 & 8. Austin Stack (left) and Cathal Brugha (right) were both critical of Collins's methods during the War of Independence. Anti-Treatyites both, Brugha would die in the Civil War, and Stack from the long-term effects of a hunger strike.

9. Michael Collins with his famous 'high nelly' bicycle, which he used to get around Dublin under the noses of Crown forces.

10. Members of 'the Squad': from left, Mick McDonnell, Liam Tobin, Vincent Byrne, Paddy Daly and Jim Slattery.

11. Tom Cullen, Michael Collins's 2nd Deputy Director of Intelligence.

12. Dave Neligan, Collins's 'spy in the Castle'. As a sergeant in the Dublin Metropolitan Police (DMP), Neligan was in a position to pass critical intelligence to the 'Big Fella'.

13. Field Marshal John French, 1st Earl of Ypres and Lord Lieutenant of Ireland, inspects members of the Royal Irish Constabulary.

14. An army sergeant points out the damage to the Lord Lieutenant's car after an unsuccessful IRA assassination attempt on John French, 19 December 1919.

15. His Majesty's forces: a member of the Dublin Metropolitan Police stands between two Auxiliaries, with a regular British soldier on the far right.

16. Head Constable Eugene Igoe. A resourceful RIC commander from Co. Mayo, Igoe was brought to Dublin to counter the activities of Collin's 'Squad', forming a plain-clothes unit that tracked, hunted down and killed members of the IRA.

17. Damaged properties in Cork, December 1920. In retaliation for an ambush of a military convoy by the IRA, Black and Tans, Auxiliaries and regular British army troops burned and looted a number of buildings in the city centre.

they attended Mass – before hastily calling off the operation after a newspaper boy recognised them and helpfully called out: 'They are not here today, gentlemen.' But perhaps another incident – one which occurred after the Squad had carried out a successful killing and run to safety, even though they were pursued by an armed and determined policeman – helps to explain the immunity. As the policeman came up to a group standing at the corner around which the Squad had just disappeared, he called out: 'Why didn't you stop them?' 'Not likely,' came the reply. 'We don't want to get what that fellow lying there got.'

The Apostles were clear-sighted – and they hunted their targets remorselessly, as the example of John Barton proves all too clearly. When one Apostle, Vincent Byrne, was being vetted for membership of the Squad, he was asked by Mick McDonnell whether he could take a life; Byrne replied that it would depend whose life was under discussion. 'Johnny Barton,' McDonnell told him – to which Byrne replied enthusiastically, 'Oh, I'd shoot him alright. He raided my house.' In fact, Barton had not only raided Byrne's house: he had also had the distinction of arresting Byrne (who was fourteen at the time) following the 1916 Rising. Byrne's crime had been to hold up two policemen, armed only with a .22 rifle. On that occasion, Byrne was allowed home because of his youth – Barton, in sharp contrast, received no such exemption. He was a G Division detective now, and his death was looming.

David Neligan, Collins's 'spy in the Castle', has left a memorable description of John Barton:

Cadaverous, immensely tall, with weird clothes and farmer's boots, he looked like a rustic from an Abbey play. Anyone would take him for a simpleton, but it would be a major error. He was easily the best detective in these islands, had plenty of touts working for him and was known to be well off financially. At that time numbers of Britons evading Conscription were hiding in Dublin [...] Johnny, with his marvellous ring of touts, quickly got on their track, the next step was to call on the reluctant warrior. It was said that, for a consideration, they were left in peace.

Collins, however, decided that Barton could not now be left in peace: Barton's activities of a political nature ordained that he must die – and so after proving his killing mettle by telling McDonnell that he wouldn't mind shooting Barton, Byrne was told the very next day, 29 November 1919, to bring his gun and report for duty that evening. Barton was to be the target of the next assassination. Byrne was accompanied by a team of three other Apostles on this hit – but as they closed on their prey, they realised that a second unit, led by Daly, was also on Barton's trail. Such a dangerous situation would seem to call into question the actual sophistication of Collins's operation – but in fact, it was the consequence of Collins's penchant for secrecy, which was so extreme that one Squad unit did not always know what another unit was up to.

On that November day, Byrne was the first to see Barton walking up Grafton Street. The detective may have realised that he was being followed, because he stopped every few paces to look at reflections in shop windows. Having spent a few moments in a Grafton Street bookshop, he then turned and began to walk the length of Grafton Street once more, again engaging in the same window-gazing routine. It was now that Byrne and his unit spotted Daly with his team on Barton's trail also – and as Byrne later recalled, it became a murderous race to see which group would get to Barton first. They were hindered, however, by the crowds of passers-by on the streets – and Barton had almost made it to the sanctuary of Brunswick Street police station before Byrne's team was able to open fire on him.

In the stiffly structured language that most of the Squad members used in recording their memoirs for the Military History Bureau, Joseph Leonard recalled: 'We experienced a grave shock when there was a heavy fusillade of firing.' His unit's shock, however, was as nothing compared to that experienced by Barton as he was shot in the back. He fell to the ground crying out: 'Oh God, what did I do to deserve this?' Nevertheless, he still possessed the strength and spirit to draw and fire his own weapon – but the Apostles were able to flee and vanish into the city. Mick McDonnell and Leonard, meanwhile, raced away from the spot but were checked on reaching College Street by a policeman who grabbed for McDonnell. Leonard recalled, 'I drew my gun and let a shout at him.' At that, understandably, the two were allowed to continue safely on their way.

Barton had been shot through the lung – and, as he lay dying, he was tended by passers-by. It was recorded that his last words were: 'They have done for me. God forgive me. What did I do? I am dying. Get me a priest.' Other people also wanted to know what Barton had done – among them Austin Stack, who asked the question of an *Irish Independent* reporter, Michael Knightley. Knightley too was a Collins associate – but all that he could find out was that Barton had been killed for 'doing political work'. It seems likely that he was shot for his part in the arrest of Hurley, after the killing of Wharton earlier that month. It has also, however, been suggested that because Barton appeared entirely unafraid of Collins, it was decided that he had to be killed so as to maintain the aura of fear that Collins's name possessed in police circles.

Such an aura of fear would certainly have been heightened by indications that the long arm of the IRA could reach to Britain, or indeed to America. I once interviewed Pa Murray, who went to New York on a mission to find and kill a man who had broken under torture and betrayed a group of Volunteers at Clonmult in County Cork. The informer had been living incognito in New York, but came out of hiding for St Patrick's Day – only to be recognised. Murray told me that he asked for and been granted the loan of an Irish policeman's revolver to kill the unfortunate informer. He was duly despatched. Such was Collins's aura: and so it is possible, even likely, that British targets would be despatched from time to time purely to maintain the psychological defences around Collins himself.

It must be stressed that the Twelve Apostles were not only used for shooting detectives, spies, and senior military and political figures. Their deadly expertise was sometimes brought to bear on civilian targets too – on targets such as Frank Brooke, the chairman of the Dublin and South Eastern Railway. In the early months of 1920, Brooke was embroiled in a particularly bitter rail strike – a dispute which also had political roots. The rail workers had refused to drive or service trains that carried or were suspected to carry what was described as 'British war material'.

Brooke was a noted Unionist: he had approved of the suppression of the Dáil, Sinn Féin and other Nationalist organisations the previous September – and now he too was placed on the hit list for the Squad. Its members now spent some time casing Brooke's County Wicklow estate – which was a nerve-wracking business: Byrne described how he and two others were sent by Tobin to Wicklow, 'unarmed, so that, if we were challenged, we were just having a spin. There was kind of a public road running through the demesne and we cycled through it. As we went along you would not know where an RIC man would appear out of the bushes. There was nothing doing here. We were only back a day or two when information was received that Brooke would be at a certain office in Westland Row.' It was the information they needed – and now they went after Brooke.

Their target was sitting in his office in the railway's headquarters at Westland Row Station in central Dublin with another railway director, Arthur Cotton, when a Squad team which included James Slattery burst into the room. Brooke tried to run, while Cotton dived under a table, thus escaping the fusillade which the assassins loosed on Brooke. Slattery recalled:

We immediately opened fire on him and he fell. As we were going down the stairs again, [Paddy] Daly said to me, 'Are you sure we got him?' I said I was not sure and Daly said, 'What about going back and making sure?' Keogh and myself went back. When I went into the room I saw a man standing at the left of the door and I fired a shot in his direction, at the same time looking across at Brooke on the floor. I fired a couple of shots at Brooke and satisfied myself that he was dead, although I did not wound the other man that was in the room. I was informed afterwards that it would have been a good job if he had been shot, as he was making himself a nuisance.

The sounds of the shots fired by the Apostles were masked by the noise made by the trains entering and leaving the nearby platforms. In addition, nobody saw, or admitted to having seen, the unmasked assassins entering or leaving the building – and the whole operation was regarded as yet another example of the Squad's deadly efficiency.

In his book *The Spy in the Castle*, David Neligan gives an example of Collins's deadliness in planning the assassination of what were in effect the rulers of Ireland at the time. Neligan had told me the story in considerably more detail in my home some years before his book was published. He was assisting me with research for my history of the IRA (1970): and in the course of our conversation, told me so many fascinating anecdotes that I persuaded him to set them down on paper; and this he duly did, writing a series of articles for the *Irish Independent*. I, of course, was editor of the *Irish Press* at this time, and was disappointed at seeing Neligan's reminiscences in a rival paper: however, I also understood that de

Valera had damaged Neligan's career so severely over the years, that Neligan could not countenance writing for my newspaper, which had after all been founded by de Valera himself. Neligan went on to use his articles as a basis for *The Spy in the Castle*, which gives the most remarkably authentic account of what it felt like to work for the British authorities in the dying days of British rule in Ireland that has ever appeared. Other people have written books based on memoirs or yellowing documents: but Neligan could truly say, 'I was there.'

Probably as many of the Squad's operations had to be called off as went ahead – and one of these abandoned hits gives such an insight into Collins's ruthlessness that Neligan – who worshipped Collins – chose not to include the vignette in his book. Sitting in my kitchen some years before he produced *The Spy in the Castle*, he painted a more flint-edged picture of Collins than he would allow ever to be represented in print. Neligan acted – among his other roles – as a bodyguard for the Dublin Recorder, Thomas O'Shaughnessy of the Privy Council – in effect a senior judge. O'Shaughnessy's daughter was marrying a British major in the Chapel Royal at Dublin Castle (the last marriage to be celebrated in that church): and the guest list read like a *Who's Who* of the establishment in Ireland. Among the guests were the then Chief Secretary Sir Hamar Greenwood; and both Irish Under-Secretaries, Sir John Anderson and Sir Alfred Cope – who, as it was later revealed, was a significant player in the swirling politics of these years. In addition to his nominal responsibilities as Under-Secretary, Cope was actually Lloyd George's man in Dublin, and was charged with conducting secret negotiations with Collins and Sinn Féin. The guest list included various generals, including Hugh Tudor, the Commander of the Black and Tans, and a whole host of other luminaries.

As this glittering wedding approached, Neligan gave the guest list to Collins whose reaction was, 'We'll plug the bloody lot of them.' The bridegroom was a major; the best man a captain: Neligan liked both of them – but nevertheless he did what he could to ensure that the 'plug' would go smoothly. The wedding took place: and in its aftermath, the Squad gathered as the wedding party made their way from the Castle to the reception at O'Shaughnessy's house in Fitzwilliam Square. We can only imagine what Neligan's state of mind must have been as he smiled and circulated amongst the guests, knowing what was to come. As the reception wore on, however, he became aware of two things. One was that none of the top political and military figures in Ireland had risked attendance at the festivities; and two, outside the house, he could see figures he recognised: there, 'pacing about in twos and threes were all the Squad and the Active Service Unit accompanied by Liam Tobin and Rory O'Connor. I went out to them. "For God's sake, go away," I said. "These fellows haven't turned up, but sent their private secretaries."' Tobin and the rest, however, refused to budge, and instead quizzed Neligan as to the identity of those present. He told them, 'Nobody but the bridegroom and a poor devil of a captain from the Duke of Wellington's regiment – the best man.' But Tobin and O'Connor were obdurate. They told Neligan that Collins had given them their orders, and they intended to proceed with them; nobody but Collins could countermand an order. In his interview with me, Vinny Byrne corroborated this. 'You got your orders,' he said. 'He was your target. That was your job and it was up to you to see that it was done, no matter how it was carried out.' With his customary blunt honesty, Byrne also summed up the Squad's attitude towards the guilt or innocence of those they shot: 'They got their orders and asked no questions.'

Confronted by the Squad's iron rules, Neligan desperately asked where Collins was to be found. They told him that he was in a café opposite Leinster House (now, of course, the home of Dáil Éireann). The location was not far from Fitzwilliam Square: not far, that is, if one is not on an errand to avert an unnecessary massacre due to take place in a few minutes' time, and is not accompanied by two of the most dangerous men in Europe, Rory O'Connor and Liam Tobin. So, with his breath in his fist (as he put it), Neligan raced to find Collins, who was not at all receptive to his news: 'Are you sure you're not going soft, Neligan?' he asked. 'I'll be on you if you are.' Neligan explained to him that the dignitaries hadn't gone to the reception, but sent their secretaries – but Collins was loathe to let the matter drop.

In his book, Neligan notes that he assured Collins that 'There was no one of a military nature present, except the best man and the bridegroom,' who had nothing to do with the British army in Ireland. The best man was, said Neligan, 'a decent fellow employed in the Allied Commission in Germany'. But Collins still wasn't satisfied. 'How do you know that?' he asked. Neligan had had the wit to take a label off the officer's luggage which he passed in the hallway as he left the O'Shaughnessy house on Fitzwilliam Square: and written on it was the name of an officer and the address of a hotel in Cologne. Neligan finished off his sanitised account in his book by recalling that 'Collins turned to Tobin and Rory: "Call off the job!" Back in the house, Tommy dished out champagne. I had a glass for the first time.'

Not every job, then, could pass off smoothly: some, like this one in Fitzwilliam Square, had to be aborted at the last minute; and indeed, it is important to emphasise this fact, lest Collins assume a superhuman form in the mind of my readers. But one 'job' which Collins did *not* call off involved the killing of an Irishman: a certain H. Quinlisk, who was one of the few Irish prisoners of war whom Roger Casement had been able to recruit in Germany for his Irish Brigade. Quinlisk had subsequently been a corporal in the Royal Irish Regiment – but on his return from the war, he was denied his back-pay for being a prisoner of war, on the grounds of his prior involvement with Casement. Quinlisk sought help from Sinn Féin – and as a result, he came to the attention of Collins, who not only gave him money, but secured a place for him at his own lodgings at 44 Mountjoy Street in Dublin's north inner city. After Quinlisk checked in there, the place was raided – but Collins seemed to have put this down, initially at least, to coincidence. He saw a potential use for Quinlisk, whose German-language skills and military training would surely come in handy.

Quinlisk, however, had other ideas. Rather than throw in his lot with Collins, he had decided instead to use his knowledge to the benefit of himself and of the British. He wrote to the 'Under Secretary, Dublin Castle', announcing that he had decided to tell all he knew about Sinn Féin and 'that scoundrel' Michael Collins, who had 'treated me scurvily'. For the next three months, the doomed Quinlisk flitted about in Sinn Féin circles, never realising that Broy had very early made known his treachery to Collins. Eventually, his time ran out – he was found dead in a ditch in County Cork in February 1920.

One of the Squad's most chilling and high-profile assassinations took place a month later. Alan Bell was a magistrate who was conducting an inquiry into Sinn Féin funds: and by March 1920, his steady, painstaking work was beginning to threaten Collins's efforts to raise a 'national loan' to fund the war effort. In addition, Bell had other responsibilities: he served on a top-level security committee which advised the Lord Lieutenant, Sir John French; and he headed a secret group which, in Bell's own words, 'picked up a good deal of useful information which leads to raids'. As Bell also reported directly to Sir Basil Thompson, the head of British intelligence at Scotland Yard, it may safely be assumed that his intelligence-gathering led to more drastic outcomes than a few police raids. The security committee on which Bell sat, had recommended that Sinn Féin 'be infiltrated with spies and some selected leaders assassinated'. Collins now tasked the Squad to mete out the same treatment to Bell.

Viewed from the perspective of almost a century later, it is difficult to understand why the British did not give Bell more protection. He lived in Monkstown in the southern suburbs of Dublin, and travelled into work daily by tram. His normal routine was to take the tram to the vicinity of Trinity College, from where he was escorted to the Castle by two detectives. Nobody appeared to realise, however, that he might be under surveillance out in the leafy suburbs. Collins learned of these clockwork movements – and took the decision to assassinate Bell not in the city centre, but in the usually tranquil environs of Ailesbury Road, a few miles south of central Dublin. A large team was assembled to carry out this most crucial job: some to wait at Ailesbury Road, others to identify the tram as it left Monkstown, before racing on bicycles to the killing scene to guide their colleagues.

The details of this killing, on 26 March 1920, highlight how such assassinations were woven into the daily life of ordinary Irish citizens. The Squad members boarded the tram, some heading upstairs, others placing themselves downstairs – where Bell, as it turned out, was also seated, without realising that two killers (Tobin and Mick McDonnell) had settled themselves just in front of him. As the tram glided past the junction of Ailesbury Road, McDonnell turned courteously and asked, 'Are you Mr Bell?' Bell, who had a bad cold, replied between fits of coughing that he was indeed. 'We want you,' McDonnell told him. The tram conductor describes what happened next:

> I noticed three men having a hold of Mr Bell. Mr Bell had his hands on either sides of the door, but the three men broke his grip, and they all came out struggling on the platform together. One of the three men was behind Mr Bell pushing him and the other two were in front. Then I noticed one of

the three men putting his hand in his pocket and taking a revolver from it. When I saw the revolver I went back to the top of the car. I passed a remark to some gentlemen that something terrible was going to happen downstairs. Then I felt very weak and sat down and saw no more.

Had the conductor not suffered from a most prudent temporary blindness, he would have seen one Squad member cutting the trolley rope to halt the tram at the end of Simmonscourt Road, and another jumping off the vehicle, before covering it with his revolver in case there might be detectives aboard. While he did so Tobin and McDonnell shot Bell – and then the Squad scattered. They left behind them a tram filled with some sixty traumatised passengers; and in Bell, most ironically, one very dead proponent of selective assassination.

The killers, however, were not quite home and dry. As they ran west up Simmonscourt Road and into Donnybrook, they realised that their environs were not quite working in their favour:

There was a great mistake made that morning. The place selected for the elimination of Bell was not very populous, with the result that we had a long distance to run before we could mingle with people and lose ourselves. We always felt very secure when a wanted man was shot in a particularly populated district because when the shooting was over, we could easily mix with the crowd and escape the watchful eye of enemy agents. Such was not the case in the shooting of

Bell. There was scarcely anybody on the road that morning, and had the enemy force had come along we would have had no chance of escaping. That was a lesson that we took deeply to heart and remembered for future occasions.

Alan Bell had been an extraordinarily busy man in the period before his death – and not least among his myriad activities was this: he had acted as handler to John Charles Byrnes, or 'Jameson', the man whom the British regarded as their best and most accomplished spy in Ireland. It is certainly true that Byrnes was a relatively successful mover on the Irish scene, and had managed to progress further into Republican circles than any other British spy before him. He had wormed his way first into the confidence of Art O'Brien, Sinn Féin's London representative, and O'Brien had then recommended him to Collins. Byrnes came to Dublin with a specific proposal: he offered to acquire large supplies of arms for the IRA – and naturally, this was a proposal which Collins found attractive. However, Byrnes was not the disaffected ex-British soldier he claimed to be – but rather an *agent provocateur* who, in the period immediately after the war, when unemployment was rife and soldiers' grievances legion, had infiltrated various left-wing movements and passed on the findings he acquired to a murky intelligence unit known as A2, which operated under a Lieutenant-Colonel Ralph Isham. The authorities eventually decided that this organisation's activities could not stand the light of day – and so it was disbanded, and in the reshuffle Byrnes was sent to Ireland.

He arrived in Dublin in December 1919 – and soon he managed to meet Collins himself, albeit at a meeting at which Byrnes's eyes were bandaged as a security measure. He was, he reported later to his superiors, impressed with the calibre of the men he met. Collins 'is the chief director of all active movement among the Sinn Féiners [...] he has taken the place of de Valera owing to the long absence of the latter. Although Collins does not take any active part in the shooting, there seems to be no doubt that he is the organiser.' Yet Byrnes too did not survive for long. It rapidly became clear that he was working for the British – for reasons outlined below, reasons which in turn led to the death of another British operative – and Collins gave orders that he should be killed. Moreover, it was decided – in spite of the lesson on assassination spots that the Squad had supposedly learned at the killing of Bell – to despatch Byrnes at another relatively quiet spot: at a place known locally as Lovers' Lane, at Ballymun on the northern fringes of Dublin. A week after Bell met his violent death, therefore, Byrnes was taken on a tram to this relatively remote spot: supposedly to meet Collins – but in fact to be told that he was a spy and was about to die. The story is that his last words before his death were: 'God bless the King. I would die for him.' Collins made Byrnes's wishes come true – but he is remembered as the agent who, though he did not succeed in capturing Collins, did at least have the distinction of meeting him and sitting down with him.

Such assassinations were not, of course, taken lightly by the authorities. Far from it: new intelligence personnel were drafted in and new thinking called for in order to revitalise the demoralised G Division detectives. Assistant Commissioner William Redmond, who was based in Belfast, was despatched to Dublin as part of this effort – and before long, Collins had made him the Squad's prime target. Remarkably, Redmond – who was staying in temporary accommodation at the Standard Hotel on Harcourt Street while an apartment was prepared for him at Dublin Castle – was accustomed to walking to work each day: and now Collins began to formulate an assassination plan.

Redmond had already managed inadvertently to draw up the death warrant of his unfortunate colleague Byrnes. On arrival in Dublin, he lined up his new staff and gave them a pep talk in which he made one fatal mistake. He told the men that they were incompetent, and he gave them a month to improve their performance before facing the sack for not capturing Collins. Unfortunately, he went on to compare these men to an operative lately arrived from London, with no experience of the Dublin scene – who had nevertheless been able to secure a meeting with Collins within a month! When the news was fed back by spies, Collins realised the identity of Byrnes instantly.

The trajectories of Collins, Byrnes and Redmond now collided with farcical results. Collins had brought Byrnes to lunch at the home of friends, the O'Connors, who lived in Donnybrook in Dublin: he wanted Mrs O'Connor, whose instincts he trusted, to assess the credibility of this new man from London. After the meal, Collins remained in the house to hear his hostess's verdict on the man who had just left in the company of Liam Tobin – and was told that Mrs O'Connor did not trust the newcomer. Meanwhile, a detective waiting outside, thinking that Tobin was

Collins, alerted a nearby raiding party that the bird had flown. They went in pursuit, but compounded their error by taking a wrong turning. Now Collins himself made off – just before the raiding party belatedly descended on the house. The leader of the raiding group was none other than Redmond himself – while one of his colleagues in the raiding party was McNamara, a crucial Collins spy in the Castle. Finding no sign of Collins, the party withdrew – with Redmond courteously apologising to Mrs O'Connor and telling her that he would not trouble her again.

Collins intended to make this wish come true also – but there was a problem to overcome: neither he nor the Squad knew what Redmond looked like. So Collins passed the word to a sergeant in the RIC, Matt McCarthy, who was stationed in the strongly Loyalist Chichester Street barracks in Belfast. McCarthy arranged that Thornton visit Belfast and – taking advantage of the fact that there was a police boxing competition taking place in the city, which almost every policeman in the barracks was attending, and that the place was virtually deserted – the pair raided a district inspector's office and stole a photograph of Redmond. Now the assassination could be planned in earnest.

It is a measure, perhaps, of how seriously the Squad took their work of killing, that Daly complained bitterly to Collins about the area he was given to stake out (closest to the Standard Hotel), because, as he told Collins, other members of the Squad would surely have shot Redmond long before he ever reached the hotel. Collins placated him, remarking that 'sometimes, the goal man sees most of the ball'. Indeed, on this occasion, Daly had little to grumble about: for on the evening in question,

21 January 1920, Redmond had got to within a few yards of the hotel when Daly suddenly recognised him and killed him with a single shot to the head – Redmond was known to be wearing a bullet-proof waistcoat. Afterwards, the gallows humour in the Squad was that Redmond had not been 'up to Standard'.

The unfortunate Byrnes and Redmond were assassinated as a result of intelligence-gathering and trap-setting – but it must be admitted that the mythic reputations of the Squad and Collins himself were sometimes burnished by sheer luck. A Captain Cecil Lees, for example, was discovered to be an agent because one of the postal raids conducted by the Crow Street team turned up a letter which showed he was engaged on intelligence work. It was later said that Lees was a noted torturer with a penchant for pulling off fingernails – and it is certainly the case that torture, up to and including heated pokers, was part and parcel of British interrogation repertoire.

At the end of March 1921, Lees too duly met his fate – though circumstances made the Squad's job rather difficult on this occasion. When Collins's men descended on Lee's lodging in St Andrew's Temperance Hotel on Wicklow Street, their prey was found to have disappeared – or at least it was thought that he had. Some of the disappointed men who had been detailed to shoot him decided to pay a visit to the cinema: and they were settled comfortably in their seats when one of them, Tom Keogh, thought that he recognised a man accompanying a lady whose features were temporarily caught in the light of the projector. They decided to follow him after the show to see where he was living – and traced him back to the same temperance hotel where he was staying with his fiancée. From their earlier study of his movements, the Apostles knew that Lees went to nearby Dublin Castle around 9am – and so were waiting for him when he emerged from the hotel the following morning. He was instantly shot down.

The Squad's highest priority target was Viceroy Lord French, and at least three unsuccessful attempts were made to kill him. The first led to no loss of life, yet it was in many ways the most remarkable. Apart from being the ambush involving the greatest number of men, it was noteworthy for the fact that several members of the Dáil volunteered to take part. In addition, it seems to have been one of the rare occasions on which Collins himself took a revolver and prepared to participate in an attack. Paddy Daly described how, in 'the late autumn of 1919, Lord French visited Trinity College one night and plans were made to ambush him coming from it'. Squad members lined the streets outside the main entrance of the college, intending to keep up a continuous fire on French before he could gain the safety of Dublin Castle. Daly notes that amongst the Dáil members who took part in the ambush were Lord Mayor of Cork Tomás Mac Curtain, together with Seán Ó'Muithuile, J. J. Walsh and Diarmuid O'Hegarty. It is not clear where Collins appeared in these *ad hoc* arrangements.

In the event, the assassination plan miscarried because French's car left not from the main entrance of Trinity College but from Lincoln Place. A second attempt on French, at the Four Courts some weeks later, was aborted because the waiting Squad expected French to be accompanied by an escort of cars. However, the Viceroy drove past the ambush in a single car accompanied by a bodyguard before Daly realised he had passed. Earlier, Collins had received information that French would be travelling to Boyle by train and that he would be met at Ashtown station, close to his official residence in north-west Dublin. The information came from a Volunteer named John Sharkey whose father was a driver on the train: passing over his intelligence, Sharkey expressed the hope that French would not be attacked on the train itself.

In fact he wasn't attacked at all, even though the ambush party included such seasoned Squad warriors as Mick McDonnell, Tom Keogh, Jim Slattery and the Tipperary mini-Squad led by Breen and Treacy. The abortive attack serves to underline a feature of the Squad's activity: the amount of planning and preparation undertaken often proved fruitless because, for some reason or another, a job had to be called off at the last moment. In this case the ambushers had cycled out to Ashtown at 5am, and in groups of two and three, so as to avoid bringing attention to themselves. French, however, seems to have had a charmed life: in this case, he made a last-minute decision not to go to Boyle by train at all, but by car.

When the attack finally did take place, on 19 December 1919, after French had taken the train on his return journey and got off at Ashtown station, his luck held yet again. French seems to have escaped because, according to Mick McDonnell, Dan Breen positioned a heavy dung cart with which it was hoped to block the road in such a way as to allow space for French's cavalcade to drive through the Squad's fusillade. French was in the first car, which the Squad had not expected: they thought that he would have been in the second car. It was realised later that the Squad had had a lucky escape: had a hand grenade not exploded prematurely, a military lorry full of soldiers would have been halted and the soldiers with their rifles would have easily outgunned the Squad.

The ambushers did succeed in halting one car and, thinking he might be shot, the driver said to Daly, 'one dead is enough'. Daly told him not to worry because the Volunteers did not shoot their prisoners: he thought the dead man the soldier was referring to was Lord French, but it turned out to be Martin Savage, a Volunteer who had heard about the proposed ambush and pleaded to be allowed to accompany the Squad at the last moment. Dan Breen was badly injured in the attack but Daly managed to get him onto his bicycle and transport the heavily built man into Dublin and a safe house. Another casualty of the raid was Mick McDonnell who, at the time of the Squad's attempt on Lord French's life – and greatly to the alarm of his comrades, was having a relationship with a policeman's daughter. The shock of Savage's death, combined with McDonnell's marital problems, brought on a temporary nervous breakdown. Tom Keogh's method of dealing with this potential security risk was to take his gun and, accompanied by Vinnie Byrne, go to the Phoenix Park, a favoured spot for lovers, in an unsuccessful search for 'this Jezebel' whom he would certainly have shot if he found her. Collins solved the problem by having McDonnell safely spirited away to the United States.

I want now to pan out a little, and to glance at the nature and scale of the forces ranged against his Apostles, the strategies they used – and the ways and means that Collins deployed to repel his enemies.

CHAPTER SIX

'A Bloody and Brutal Anarchy'

A still from a British newsreel purporting to show Sinn Féiners shot dead by Auxiliaries in Co. Kerry. The photograph in fact shows a street in Killiney in the suburbs of Dublin.

I N LONDON, THE BRITISH GOVERNMENT OF DAVID LLOYD George watched these 'Apostolic administrations' and the unravelling security situation in Ireland with disbelief and alarm. Collins seemed untouchable at home; in the United States, meanwhile, de Valera's activities were shifting the public mood away from Britain and in favour of Republican Ireland. This was disturbing in itself: the Great War was now concluded, but it was becoming clear that the balance of power in the world was shifting decisively; and no British government could afford any longer to discount the United States, or to leave the American people out of its political calculations. At the same time, Lloyd George continually had to reckon also with powerful conservative figures on the domestic front, who were irrevocably hostile to the claims of Irish nationalism. There was, for example, the ever-present negativism of such Unionist figures as Carson, who as late as 1918 had continued to sit in the cabinet – and who in 1919, with the country clearly crying out for a political solution, warned Lloyd George that if any renewed Home Rule proposals should threaten the status of Ulster, he would put the illegal Ulster Provisional Government into effect and place the Ulster Volunteer Force on a war footing.

As for the enigmatic Lloyd George himself: whether the Prime Minister would or would not have been personally sympathetic to Irish Nationalist claims is a moot point. Later, during the fraught Treaty negotiations of 1921, Lloyd George would acknowledge to Collins that he would have hanged him had he had the opportunity of doing so; and on an earlier occasion, in November 1920, he announced gleefully that the government, through its use of state-sponsored violence in Ireland, had 'murder by the throat' (see page 210). At all stages, however, it is crucial to remember that the Welshman was a pragmatist, ensuring that his Castle officials continued – through Alfred Cope – to manage underground contacts with Collins and Sinn Féin, while still continuing his policy of 'frightfulness': wholesale extrajudicial violence directed at both life and property throughout the country.

Now, in the dark days of 1920, the tactics of both sides came to mirror each other. On the British side, the retarding influence of the Unionists and the hardline Conservatives in the corridors of power at Westminster stayed Lloyd George's hand in bringing forward any measure of Home Rule that would have placated Nationalist Ireland; and more and more directed the British effort towards underground counter-insurgency methods wherein unacknowledged Squad tactics were used. Tactics on both sides became bloodier and more violent – so much so that the *Daily Chronicle*, controlled by Lloyd George, was able to declare in January 1920 that revenge politics might, as a result of activities in Ireland, become the norm: 'It is obvious that, if these murderous clubs pursue their cause much longer, we may see counter clubs springing up and the lives of prominent Sinn Féiners becoming as unsafe as prominent officials.'

This particular editorial had been provoked by the shooting, a few days earlier, of a policeman in Thurles, County Tipperary; his colleagues, aided by the military, retaliated by running amok in the town. In addition, January saw the beginnings of widespread assaults on fortified RIC barracks in Ireland, including three in Cork alone. Additional areas – Kilkenny, Waterford and Wexford – were placed under martial law, as attacks modelled on the Cork onslaught spread through surrounding counties. Cork, indeed, had become a centre of Republican activity: the Lord Mayor of Cork, Tomás Mac Curtain, and the deputy Lord Mayor and Sinn Féin TD, Terence Mac Swiney, pressed Collins to stage a series of what were called 'revolving risings', modelled on 1916. These would have involved the seizure of a strong point in one part of the country in one week, holding out for as long as possible, and then going down in a blaze of glory while another district took up the baton.

The barracks attacks, like the rest of the armed struggle, naturally depended on the support of the people – and reports from two of the top intelligence leaders in the IRA, Florence O'Donoghue in Cork and Frank Thornton in Dublin, indicated that the people were indeed now solidly behind such militant policies. They acted as the fighting men's eyes and ears, shielding them from their enemies and making it possible for the guerrillas to continue to fight. This civilian support showed

itself politically too – specifically in the results of Irish munici-
pal elections held in January 1920, when Sinn Féin won 172 of
Ireland's 206 councils.

By now the Unionists in Ulster were squaring up to the idea
that, while Partition was now a distinct possibility in Ireland,
they would only be able to control six of that province's nine
counties. Demographic calculations left them in no doubt as to
the facts: Counties Cavan, Donegal and Monaghan held large
Catholic and Nationalist majorities, and so could not be possibly included in any new Unionist-majority statelet; Counties
Fermanagh and Tyrone also held Nationalist majorities – but
here, the margins were more slender, and could be balanced
by large Unionist populations in Belfast and across Counties
Down and Antrim. Derry city too was a Nationalist stronghold
– but the city's symbolism and the history of the seventeenth-
century Siege of Derry, when the Protestants of the city had
held out against a Catholic King James, meant that Derry could
not readily be handed over to any looming new Irish state.
Lines were being drawn that would soon become manifest.

Throughout the rest of Ireland, and with the force of the
ballot box behind them, newly elected Sinn Féin councils began
declaring their allegiance to the Dáil and not the Castle – and
now the British undercover intelligence network decided that
it was time to shout *Stop*. In Cork, the British were of course
aware that both Mac Curtain and Mac Swiney were active
in the IRA – and on 16 March 1920, Mac Curtain received a
death notice written on Dáil Éireann notepaper which had been
seized by the police during a raid on Sinn Féin headquarters

on Harcourt Street in Dublin. It said: 'Tomás Mac Curtain: prepare for death. You are doomed.' Other prominent Sinn Féin figures received similar notices. The idea behind the note-paper, of course, was to have it thought that the Sinn Féiners intended murdering each other. Four days after Mac Curtain received his note, another policeman was shot dead outside Cork. Now, the stage set, a revenge British intelligence opera-tion swung into action: a police cordon was thrown around Mac Curtain's home – and, at about one o'clock in the morning of 20 March, a party of armed men with blackened faces forced their way into the house and shot Mac Curtain dead in the presence of his wife and children.

Mac Curtain's death prompted a fierce exchange in the pro-paganda war, which the Irish won hands-down. Lloyd George and the British administration under Lord French sought to gain favourable publicity with claims that Mac Curtain had been murdered by fellow Sinn Féiners. The police selected the coroner's jury, but despite this the jury's verdict was:

WE find that Alderman Tomás Mac Curtain, Lord Mayor of Cork, died from Shock and Haemorrhage, caused by bullet wounds, and that he was wilfully wounded under circumstances of the most callous brutality and that the murder was organised and carried out by the RIC officially directed by the British Government.

We return a verdict of wilful murder against David Lloyd George, Prime Minister of England, Lord French, Lord Lieutenant of Ireland; Ian McPherson, Late Chief

Secretary of Ireland; Acting Inspector General Smith of the RIC, Divisional Inspector Clayton of the RIC, D.I. Swanzy and some unknown members of the RIC.

Mac Swiney was elected in Mac Curtain's place as Lord Mayor of Cork, and he marked the occasion by saying that 'We do not abrogate our function to demand and see the evildoers and murderers are punished for their crimes.' As we will see, the murderers *were* punished and very serious consequences ensued – but for now, the policy of murdering senior Nationalist officials continued. A former Lord Mayor of Limerick, George Clancy, was murdered during curfew hours. A leading Irish Nationalist, Joseph O'Donoghue, was also shot – and it is clear that many regular British army officers found this kind of activity difficult to stomach. General Hubert Gough, who six years previously had led the threatened Curragh mutiny, wrote:

> Law and order have given way to a bloody and brutal anarchy [...] England has departed further from her own standards and further from the standards even of any nation in the world, not excepting the Turk and Zulu, than has ever been known in history before.

It was, however, on brutal tactics that the British authorities now began consistently to rely. A new military commander was appointed in Ireland: General Sir Neville Macready, whose career already demonstrated a familiarity with the principles of harsh reality. Macready had served as a tough-minded

Commissioner of London's Metropolitan Police; and in 1910, had shown a heavy-handed ruthlessness towards striking Welsh miners at Tonypandy. It might be noted, however, that he had made no known objections to Unionist threats during the Home Rule Crisis.

Operating alongside Macready was Hugh Tudor, who was now appointed as head of what was described as a reconstituted police force – and a body which would pass into Irish history as the hated 'Black and Tans'. They were named for a celebrated Irish hunt, though in truth they owed their nickname to the fact that their uniform was an amalgam of black and tan army and police tunic and trousers. In August 1920, the Castle would publish a laudatory testament to the Black and Tans, noting that:

> They did not wait for the usual uniform, they came at once. They were wanted badly and the RIC welcomed them. They know what danger is. They have looked Death in the eyes before and did not flinch. They will not flinch now. They will go on with the job – the job of making Ireland once again safe for the law-abiding, an appropriate hell for those whose trade is agitation and whose method is murder.

These Black and Tans were for the most part ex-servicemen who had fought in the Great War; some of them were Irish and they were paid ten shillings a day. Their record in Ireland – a list of their activities includes murders, house burnings, sackings of towns and random shootings – does them no credit; yet they formed an integral part of what was known as the 'Police War'. The reasoning behind their formation, meanwhile, was this: the British – and in particular such figures as Field Marshal Sir Henry Wilson – did not want to be viewed in the eyes of the world as putting down an independence movement supported at the ballot box by a majority of the population. Instead, therefore, the public relations effort was directed at making it appear that Britain was engaged against an explicitly *criminal* movement.

The formation of the Tans was accompanied by the creation of another force – officially described as the Auxiliary Police Cadets so as to maintain the anti-crime motif. The 'Auxis', as they were speedily christened, comprised ex-officers who were paid a pound a day. In Ireland, the 'Auxis' are remembered for baulking at neither overt nor clandestine murder, and for the calculated use of torture. In his statement to the Bureau of Military History, David Neligan describes the hundred or so Auxiliaries of 'F' Company, a unit with a particularly bad reputation. These were quartered in the Upper Yard at Dublin Castle, where he was able to observe their unprepossessing comings and goings.

They were an extraordinary collection. I saw [...] Highlanders, complete in kilt, naval officers, cowboys and types from every quarter of the globe. A sprinkling of the crowd wore the blue tunic of the RIC with the letters 'T.C.' [temporary cadets]. All wore Glengarry caps, some old British Army uniforms [...] the canteen did a roaring trade night and day. Once, when cash ran out, a squad raided the City Hall in broad daylight and stole several thousand pounds. Night after night a dark tall fellow wearing a colonel's epaulette and a Glengarry cap was frog-marched to a lorry by his men. He was so drunk that he could not proceed under his own steam, but at the same time insisted on going out to look for 'the damn Shinners'.

Neligan's description helps to explain the numbers of people shot by such Auxiliaries while 'trying to escape'. One of the reasons that helped them to get away with the sort of behaviour mentioned by Neligan was that 'these fellows had a different name for every day of the week' – in short, that they were as difficult to identify as to control. Another source, on the other hand, described these men in ecstatic terms: this was Caroline Woodcock, the wife of a British military official stationed in Ireland, and a canny if thoroughly prejudiced observer of the scene. For Woodcock, the men of the Auxiliaries were a delightful sight:

> The most awe-inspiring sight for me was the carloads of Auxiliaries, eight or ten splendid-looking men [...] armed to the teeth and flying a large Black and Tan flag. On the Tan half a large 'B' was painted and on the black bit the letter 'T' [...] the colours of the only force that since the days of Cromwell has ever ruled Ireland.

To be sure, it is likely that Cromwell would have had little cause to complain about the methods of these men.

Two separate shootings around this time exemplify the underground and bloody nature of this so-called 'Police War' – and also proved to have violent repercussions in Ulster. Neither shooting was especially concerned with the Squad, although each certainly grew out of the same Collins intelligence tree from which the Squad itself also sprouted. One was the response to Mac Curtain's killing; and the other was a response to the killing of a Colonel Smyth of the RIC.

An intelligence report which reached Collins on 20 July 1920 demonstrated to his satisfaction how the picture of those involved in the Mac Curtain murder was put together:

Head Constable Cahill came to Monaghan about three weeks after the murder of Thom. Mac Curtain. He came from King Street Barracks, Cork, and was escorted by four armed policemen. One of his guards remarked to one of the older men in Monaghan Barracks: 'He (Cahill) is a good man. He is not afraid of them (the Volunteers).' One of his children (about 10 years old) remarked in the barracks a short time after they came, 'When I grow up I won't murder Lord Mayors.' He (Cahill) passed various remarks [...] about the proper way to suppress sedition, and said the proper way to do so, was to shoot them down. From this and various remarks he made he gave me the impression he had to do with the murder of Thos. Mac Curtain.

From such snippets as these, Collins determined that a key figure in the shooting of Mac Curtain was a District Inspector

Oswald Swanzy, who, for his own safety, had been transferred from Cork to the security of heavily Unionist Lisburn in County Antrim. At first, Collins planned to give the job of killing Swanzy to the Apostles – but later, local loyalties trumped these earlier plans, and he opted to give the task (or honour) to a group drawn from Mac Curtain's own IRA brigade. One of the five chosen was Sean Culhane, who was at the time still in his teens. Culhane later recalled Collins's suggestion that the job was too much for so young a lad, and that 'it should be carried out by experienced men, from Dublin'.

Culhane, however, objected vigorously: he had his orders from Cork, he said, and this was by rights a Cork Brigade job. Since Collins was himself a Corkman, he could understand such a response: he eventually chose to delegate this particular responsibility to Cathal Brugha, as Minister for Defence – and, after quizzing Culhane, Brugha gave him the go-ahead. It was decided that Culhane would fire the first shot and that he would use Mac Curtain's own gun. (Ironically, another IRA man, Jim Grey, by pretending to be a Loyalist, had secured a permit for the gun from Swanzy himself.)

The target and date (August 1920) were set and the plans were in progress – and now it was decided that the hit team must include Ulster members, so that a profusion of Cork accents would not put the team under suspicion in Lisburn. The first effort to kill Swanzy had to be abandoned because a taxi which the group hired and then hijacked, broke down. The would-be assassination team retreated to the relative safety of nearby Belfast – and were then ordered to return south because the Belfast leader, Joe McKelvey, correctly decided that the dangers of having too many Cork people in Ulster remained – quite simply, they were drawing attention to themselves every time they opened their mouths. The hit was placed on hold – though only for a week, until 20 August, when two would-be assassins returned to Lisburn to try again. This time, they planned to take Swanzy out as he emerged from a church service.

This time the assassins used a taxi owned by a Volunteer, Sean Leonard, who was under orders to tell the police that his taxi had been hijacked. The vehicle was parked about two hundred yards from the church with the engine running. Swanzy duly emerged from the church as expected. He was accompanied by his father and by an army major. Roger McCorley, a prominent Belfast IRA leader who had been scouting the killing ground, took part in the bloody episode. The major and Swanzy's father were knocked to either side from the rear as Culhane approached: Culhane shot Swanzy behind the right ear, killing him instantly as the bullet travelled through his head exiting between his ear and eye. The other Corkman, Dick Murphy, shot Swanzy immediately after Culhane. McCorley remembered that, 'We all opened fire on him [...] when we were satisfied that the execution had been carried out, we started off for the taxi.'

The assassins, however, were pursued by an angry crowd – and so McCorley stopped to fire at them, too. 'This left me a considerable way behind the others. I was then attacked by an ex-British officer called Woods who seemed to have plenty of courage. Although I was carrying a revolver in my hand, he attacked me with a blackthorn stick and by a fluke I shot the stick out of his hand. When I got within twenty yards of the car, it started off and I was unable to make the necessary speed to catch it.' However, the taxi was only able to attain a top speed of around thirty miles an hour, and as McCorley continued to run after it, one of the team – Tom Fox of Belfast – realised that McCorley was not in the taxi and asked Leonard to stop. In what could have been a fatal comedy of errors, McCorley reached the taxi on one side and jumped into the back seat just as Fox jumped out on the other side to look for him. The jump probably saved his life, however, for as McCorley jumped into the taxi, the car jerked forward – and he inadvertently fired his revolver, putting a bullet through the seat out of which Fox had just jumped.

Another detail which might have had fatal consequence for the raiding party was the fact that they had forgotten to disable the vehicle the police were using – yet another taxi. The police taxi made better speed than the assassins' vehicle – and in fact was catching up rapidly when it happened to take a corner too fast and lost two tyres. The assassins, then, were able to safely get out of Lisburn and into Belfast, where they boarded a train bound for Dublin. As it passed through Lisburn on its way south, they saw that a number of houses were on fire. These fires marked the commencement of a pogrom directed against Catholics in many parts of Ulster: thirty-one people were killed in the weeks that followed, and more than two hundred injuries were reported in Lisburn, Banbridge and Belfast. The injury list was most likely far larger, but there is a well-established tradition in what was soon to become Northern Ireland: some Catholics avoided attending Protestant hospitals. Be that as it may, it is still possible a century later to meet Ulster Catholics who regard the Swanzy and Smyth killings as marking the rebirth of something frightful: the sleeping volcano of Ulster sectarianism.

The killing of Ulsterman Lieutenant Colonel Bruce Smyth, indeed, is regarded by many commentators as probably even more significant than that of Mac Curtain. Smyth was Commissioner of the RIC in Munster; he was also renowned in his native Ulster as being the holder of a Victoria Cross – and he carried additional significance too, for he was the first to publicly spell out the fact that the British government were sponsoring a 'shoot to kill' policy in Ireland. He did this before an audience of RIC men at Listowel Barracks in County Kerry on 19 June 1920, thereby both precipitating his own death and triggering a mutiny in the RIC. This corps, as we know, was already under heavy moral and physical pressure – but the officer's remarks so inflamed some of the men that they mutinied on the spot. The colonel had delivered the following highly significant address:

Well men, I have something to tell you, something I am sure you would not want your wives to hear. Sinn Féin has had all the sport up to the present and we are going to have it now [...] We must take the offensive and beat Sinn Féin at its own game. Martial Law applying to all Ireland is to come into operation immediately. In fact, we are to have our scheme of amalgamation completed on June 21st. I am promised as many troops from England as I require, thousands are coming in daily.

If a police barracks is burned, or if the barracks occupied is not suitable, then the best house in the locality is to be commandeered, the occupants thrown out into the gutter, let them lie there, the more the merrier. Police and military will patrol the country at least five times a week, they are not to confine themselves to the main roads, but make across the country, lie in ambush and when civilians are seen approaching shout 'up hands': should the order not be obeyed at once, shoot and shoot to kill. If the persons approaching carry their hands in their pockets or are in any way suspicious-looking, shoot them down. You may make mistakes occasionally, and innocent persons may be shot but that cannot be helped, and you are bound to get the right person sometime. The more you shoot, the better I shall like you, and I assure you that no policemen will get into trouble for shooting a man. Hunger strikers will be allowed to die in jail – the more the better. Some of them have already died and a damn bad job they were not all allowed to die. As a matter of fact some of them have already been dealt with in a manner their friends will never know about. An emigrant ship left an Irish port for a foreign one with lots of Sinn Féiners on board; I assure you men it will never reach port.

We want you to carry out this scheme and wipe out Sinn Féin. Any man who is not prepared to do this is a hindrance and had better leave the job at once.

It would be interesting to find out just what was involved in Smyth's notion of a ship's sinking. For some years, this was thought to be a reference to the *Viknor*, the loss of which was never definitively explained: it was said to have hit a mine en route to Norway, with six mysterious men described as stowaways in the casualty lists. However, the *Viknor* went down in 1915, some years before Smyth's harangue in Listowel – and so we are left to wonder whether there was indeed information in circulation in British intelligence circles that a ship was to be sunk with British connivance – and presumably British seamen aboard. A dispatch from the Intelligence chief Captain R. C. Hall, which was intercepted by Collins, contains the following: 'I am afraid the *Viknor* has gone down. She had some very important prisoners on board and I badly wanted their papers.' So: were the six stowaways on the *Viknor* in fact prisoners? If they were, why was the British ship taking them to Norway – and how did it come to sink? The *Viknor* and the mysterious ship referred to by Smyth are just two of the many dimly glimpsed occurrences that hide behind a fog of undercover intelligence warfare.

What we *do* know – and in fact, it underlines the official nature of Smyth's address in Listowel that day – is the fact that the British officer who accompanied him as he spoke, was none other than General Hugh Tudor, the head of the newly formed Black and Tans. It was now clear: a new British counter-insurgency move was being officially signalled. But something else was also clear: the immediate RIC reactions were horror – and rebellion. One of Smyth's listeners, a Constable Jeremiah Mee, now stepped forward and said: 'By your accent, I take it that you are an Englishman, and in your ignorance you forget that you are addressing Irishmen.' Mee then removed his cap belt and his arms, laid them on the table in front of Smyth, and said, 'These too are English, take them and go to hell with you, you murderer.' Smyth ordered that the mutinous Mee be arrested immediately – but the other RIC men refused, and by a show of arms demonstrated to the startled and furious Smyth exactly where their loyalties lay. Several of the men were dismissed. But worse was to befall Smyth: a month after he spoke that day at Listowel, a Cork IRA squad entered the country club at Cork. One of the men identified Smyth and spoke to him, saying: 'Your orders were to shoot on sight: you are in sight now. So make ready.' Smyth was then shot dead.

At this stage it is worth noting that it was not only the Dublin and Cork IRAs which were in possession of Squads; the fact was that the IRA had units at its disposal in every county in Ireland. And others followed: for the British would in due course establish a 'Squad' of their own. This development was the brainchild of Eugene Igoe, a tough-minded but courteous and remarkably handsome commander of the RIC in County Mayo who was drafted in specifically to organise efficient resistance to Collins in Dublin. Details – harvested years later by the Irish Bureau of Military History, and preserved since

– show the Squad's effort to track and kill Igoe and his men. They also provide a glimpse of the strain these men were under as they went about their business. These records have a unique quality of their own: the mundane language used by Squad members could easily deceive, if one did not already know the details of their 'business'. After all, a comment such as 'We eventually caught up with them in Harcourt Street and did the job,' could easily refer to an activity such as photography rather than the business of killing.

This 'business' was imprinted on the memories of these men decades later. Their statements were taken over a quarter of a century after the events described – but the strong imprint of exactly what routes they took on their lethal missions (be they successful or not) illustrates the fact that behind the language lay both heightened tension stress and a familiarity – a psychogeography of sorts – of the Dublin streets they navigated. In addition, Igoe's *modus operandi* was similar to the Squad's own. He and his unit, which were drawn from the RIC, moved about the streets in groups dressed in plain clothes, separated from each other by a few paces so that they did not appear to be an organised gang. Their mission – a mirror mission – was to identify and capture, or kill, IRA men. The RIC men, like the Squad itself, escaped identification partly because of their evasive tactics, and partly because, like Igoe himself, they came from the country and were not known in Dublin.

The two parties of men wove intricate patterns through the streets of the city. Frank Thornton described how on different occasions the gang was located by IRA intelligence officers and word sent to the Squad to come and eliminate them. Yet invariably, Igoe and his men evaded death by doubling back on their tracks so that the Squad would lose them. On one occasion when the Squad had come upon Igoe's party, an unexpected army patrol emerged from a side street. The inimitable Vinnie Byrne greeted their appearance with a snatch from a popular song of the time: *Do I want to see my mammie again? I do.* The rest of the Squad agreed with him and decamped immediately. Igoe and his men always operated with a patrol or an armoured car somewhere in the vicinity – and a blast on a whistle would speedily bring aid.

One of the tactics Igoe and his men deployed was that of courtesy. When they stopped a suspect, all passers-by would observe were a couple of men talking politely to someone who was just apparently another passer-by or perhaps an acquaintance. Another factor which enabled Igoe to keep ahead of the Squad was the fact that, like Collins, his adversaries didn't have a photograph of him. In an effort to rectify this, Crow Street brought a Galway Volunteer, Thomas Newel – who knew Igoe from Galway – to Dublin. For several weeks Newel walked the streets of Dublin, fruitlessly trying to pick up Igoe's trail. He did spot him in the distance once or twice, but Igoe was always gone before the Squad could arrive.

Then, on 7 January 1921, Newel spotted his quarry. In Squad-speak, he recorded in his Military Bureau statement what happened next – and we can see how easily it could have ended in a bloodbath. Newel picked up their trail at Sackville Street and followed then to Dame Street – and, he continued:

They crossed Dame Street into Trinity Street and into Wicklow Street. In Wicklow Street I met Charlie Dalton and told him that Igoe and his gang had gone into Grafton Street. We both went back to Headquarters on Crow St where he reported the matter.

Having alerted Crow Street – which in turn alerted the Squad – Dalton decided that Igoe was probably heading for Harcourt Street railway station to observe the comings and goings. So he decided to head for nearby St Stephen's Green with Newel to wait for the Squad. They gathered – and even forty years later, Byrne would remember what he claimed were Tobin's exact words on finding they had no weapons: 'For God's sake, get them quick: Igoe is on his way to Harcourt railway station.' Keogh chimed in: 'Go and get the guns and we will meet you in Stephen's Green,' he said to Byrne. Byrne recalled:

I made a dash down the stairs and away over to the [weapons] dump at Morelands I collected the guns. Jimmy's long Webley, Tom's Peter and short Webley and my own Peter. Tom Keogh always carried a Webley in case his Peter would jam. I buckled on my belt beneath my dustcoat and slung the guns which were all in holsters, leaving the dump I proceeded to Liffey Street and crossed the metal bridge.

But as Byrne headed for St Stephen's Green, he was unaware that Igoe had apprehended Charlie Dalton and Newel. Charlie

Dalton's account continues the saga – again with meticulous recall of street names and landmarks:

Newel and I proceeded to Grafton Street by the shortest route and when we had almost reached Weir's jewellery stores, I noticed that we had been passed by some men who I instinctively recognised as Igoe's party, although Newel had not had time to confirm this. When they had passed us out, they wheeled on us. I felt a hand gripping the collar of my coat; I turned to see who was holding me. It was Igoe. 'Come on, Newel,' he said. 'I want you.'

Frantically Dalton replied, 'My name is not Newel!' 'I know you anyway,' said Igoe – and ordered his arrest. Pedestrians passed by all the while, unaware that anything unusual was happening. Dalton and Newel were ordered to walk down Trinity Street towards Suffolk Street until they came to 18 Dame Street, which was an insurance office. Insurance was something the two IRA men needed badly at that moment. Newel and Dalton were ordered to stand against a wall some yards apart so that they could not hear each other's answer as Igoe questioned them.

Now Vinnie Byrne entered the picture. Dalton spotted him crossing Dame Street en route to St Stephen's Green. Byrne's statement recalls:

As I was crossing Dame Street I noticed a group of men standing along the wall and speaking to two of them was

Charlie Dalton. I did not know any of the men and I thought to myself that the group was probably the Southside ASU. I carried on up Dame Street, as I was passing Charlie I gave him a slight nod of my head. He did not recognise me. I thought it was strange. When I arrived at Stephen's Green I met the remainder of the Squad and Intelligence. I told Tom Keogh that I had seen Charlie in Dame Street with some fellas but I did not know any of them. As far as I can remember we proceeded to Harcourt Street but there was no sign of Igoe or his gang or anybody looking like his party.

There was a good reason for this; Igoe was still back in Dame Street interrogating Newel and Dalton, who recalled that 'in reply to the questions put to me I gave my correct name and address. I stated that I was a believer in Home Rule and that my father was a Justice of the Peace and did not agree with the Sinn Féin policy.' Igoe asked Dalton how he came to know the other man and Dalton replied that he didn't know him, that he had just been stopped on the street and asked for directions.

At this point, however, Newel lost his patience with Igoe's questioning and burst out: 'I know you, Igoe – and you know me.' Now the interrogations stopped: Dalton was told to go and warned not to look back. He said:

I walked on in the direction of Trinity Street knowing from the footsteps behind me that I was under cover of some of Igoe's men. I moved fairly slowly at first, not being physically able to go any faster. I moved through Trinity Street,

Suffolk Street and into Wicklow Street, gaining a few yards on each bend and when I turned the corner of Wicklow Street, made a dash of about 30 or 40 yards and entered a building where my father had his commercial offices. I went up to the two flights of stairs into his office and was practically in a state of collapse upon reaching it. My father's typist was in the office but I did not speak to her as I expected to hear the sound of steps on the stairs any second. After about 5 minutes, as nothing happened, I asked her to put on her hat and coat and accompany me, which she did. We walked out from the office and up Clarendon Street as far as St Stephen's Green, where I parted with my pilot and located the Squad. Having told Tom Keogh what happened, I got hold of a gun and we all returned to Dame Street in the hope of over taking some of Igoe's party. We searched several streets in the area without coming across them. We assumed that they must have entered the Castle as they were nowhere to be seen.

Meanwhile Newel had been directed to walk to an inconspicuous thoroughfare [Greek Street, north of the river Liffey], with two of Igoe's men in front, two behind and one on either side. Here Igoe resumed his questioning, asking Newel what he was doing in Dublin. Newel refused to answer: then Igoe told him to run into Greek Street. Encircled by Igoe's men, the courageous Newel looked Igoe in the eye and said: 'If you want to shoot me, shoot me where I am standing.' Igoe replied by giving Newel a hell of a punch which sent me several yards into the street and immediately opened fire on me. I fell, and I was not able to get up as I had received four bullet wounds, one in the calf of the right leg, two in the right hip and one flesh wound in the stomach. I then saw Igoe blow a whistle. Within a minute a police van arrived. I was put roughly in it and taken to the Bridewell [police station]. I was questioned as to where I lived in Dublin. I refused to tell them. I was beaten on the head with the butt end of a revolver, four of my teeth were knocked out and three of four others broken. I was left lying on the floor for some hours and then taken by ambulance to George VI hospital.

Newel subsequently spent years in hospital and was crippled for life.

It is difficult to encapsulate Igoe's impact on the Irish scene, although it is safe to say that it was minor in comparison to that of the Apostles. Certainly Igoe was treated well by the authorities. What struck me on sifting through the Chief Secretary's archival papers, and what strikes me now, was the speed with which a request to give Igoe a pension was dealt with, and the generosity of the award in the context of the time. The application was passed within a matter of days – and when it came before the Whitehall Tribunal, which decided on compensation for activities such as those of Igoe, it was stated:

[...] considerable attention to Head Constable Igoe's case. Colonel Winter gave evidence on Igoe's behalf and emphasised the H-C's loyalty and devotion to duty and his quite exceptional danger which may involve him in frequent removals from one part of the globe to another. The Tribunal also saw Igoe himself; he created a favourable impression. One feature of hardship is that Igoe will never be able to return to a forty-three-acre farm in Ireland to which he had hoped to retire when he left the RIC. Colonel Winter considers fifteen hundred the least that Igoe deserves. He suggests annuity and lump sum...

If one sets the £1500 pension awarded to Igoe against the fact that the Auxiliaries and Black and Tans received only one pound and ten shillings a day respectively, his settlement can be seen to be highly significant. It is said that a condition of the settlement was that Igoe should be able to draw his reward anywhere in the world under cloak of anonymity. This was not because, as one might assume, he lived a life perpetually on the run from the vengeance of the IRA, but because he in fact continued to work undercover for the British in various parts of the globe.

The fact remains, of course, that the British authorities – try though they might, and in a variety of ways – could not keep up with Collins, nor match his methods, skill and speed. They did of course try their best: so let us look now at the most successful among their number, and at the strategies – some of them horrifying – that were set in place to try to catch their quarry.

CHAPTER SEVEN

'It Baffles Description…'

The sack of Balbriggan: the remains of a row of houses in Clonard Street after Black and Tans burned the quiet Co. Dublin town, November 1920.

THE BRITISH RESPONSE TO THE EFFORTS OF COLLINS and his colleagues was marked by differences of method, of personnel and of class; and was frequently riven by intense inter-departmental rivalry. The intelligence work of educated men contrasted sharply with the violent methods of the Black and Tans, who have undoubtedly earned their infamous place in Irish history, and of the Auxiliaries, whose behaviour was (if such a thing is possible) even worse. In his *Michael Collins: A Life* (1996), James Mackay has described the Auxiliaries thus:

> They wore their medal ribbons with fierce pride and included many a military cross and Distinguished Service order. They were the product of the finest English public schools and a good percentage of them came from old Anglo-Irish families: but otherwise they differed only from the Black and Tans in their ruthlessness and ferocity, utterly fearless, especially when cornered, they often earned the respect of their opponents, but they also included a sinister sprinkling of sadists and psychopaths who delighted in devising ever more fiendish methods of torture, mutilation and death.

This description is no exaggeration. One favoured Auxiliary technique, devised when a parent or a group of adults was to be shot, was to place tin buckets on the heads of any children on the scene: this technique was crude but effective, hindering as it did any potential outcry and removing the possibility of eye-witnesses to the crime or crimes. The Auxiliaries also deployed various forms of torture – flogging boys to secure informa-tion, for example – as standard procedure – as was revealed in the report of the American Commission on Conditions in Ireland of 1921. Indeed, the American intelligence expert J. B. E. Hittle, a former US undercover operative, has compared certain methods of the Auxiliaries to those of the 'German Order Police battalions against Jews in Lithuania, Poland and the Ukraine in the summer of 1941'. In his *Michael Collins and the Anglo-Irish War: Britain's Counter-Insurgency Failure*, Hittle writes that in Ireland 'the highly mobile truck-mounted British Auxiliaries conducted more than a dozen disturbingly similar clearing actions in Irish communities between July 1920 and July 1921'. Essentially, I would suggest that the Auxiliaries went about like Wild West gunmen, although better armed. Apart from two-holstered .45 revolvers, they carried carbines and had machine guns mounted on their armoured cars.

The force certainly presented a formidable enemy for the lightly armed Squad, who achieved little success against them – yet their tactics undid any military success they achieved. It is certainly the case that the Auxiliaries' methods, espe-cially when viewed alongside those of the Black and Tans, were highly counterproductive. Even some of their own members were revolted by their behaviour. A letter to his mother from an Auxiliary, dated 16 December 1920, is illuminating in this respect. The cadet in question described himself as being in bed recovering from a chill – which he had caught the previous Saturday night when an attempt ('in which I took a reluctant part') was made by the force to burn Cork city centre:

> We did it alright never mind how much the well-intentioned Hamar Greenwood would excuse us. In all my life I have never experienced such orgies of murder, arson and looting as I have witnessed during the past 16 days with the RIC Auxiliaries. It baffles description. And we are supposed to be officers and gentlemen. There are quite a number of decent fellows and likewise a lot of ruffians. On our arrival here one of our heroes held up a car with a priest and civilian in it and shot them through the head without cause or provocation. We were very kindly received by the people but the consequences of this cold-blooded murder is that no one will come within a mile of us now and all shops are closed. [...] Many who witness similar scenes in France and Flanders say that nothing they have experienced was comparable to the punishment meted out to Cork...

The boot boys of the Black and Tans, meanwhile, kept Sir Hamar Greenwood just as busy defending the indefensible in the House of Commons. To give just one example: following a pub fight in Balbriggan in which two Tans were shot, their comrades went on the rampage – burning a hosiery factory, forty-nine houses and four public houses, and killing two local people. Sir Hamar told the Commons that it was 'impossible' to find out who, of the 250-odd Tans who had broken out of their barracks to take part, was responsible for the rampage. Nor could anything be done about similar rampages in the towns of Ennistymon, Lahinch and Milltown Malbay in which four people were killed, and scores of buildings destroyed.

Other towns, including Fermoy, Thurles, Lismore and Mallow, were also extensively damaged – and even Sir Henry Wilson became appalled at what was taking place in the name of the crown. Like Macready, head of the army in Ireland, Wilson was motivated not by humanitarian considerations but rather by concern at what the licence given to the new corps was doing to the morale and discipline of the regular army. He proposed that the government should take responsibility for the shootings by drawing up a list of prominent Sinn Féiners and then shooting them by roster whenever an IRA attack occurred. Not surprisingly Lloyd George, who already had enough trouble dealing with the bad publicity arising from the 'frightfulness' policy, 'fairly danced' at this proposal and rejected Wilson's helpful suggestion. The army general nominally in charge of the Auxiliaries, Frank Percy Crozier, eventually resigned in protest over the behaviour of his men and the obstacles put in his way in attempting to discipline them. It is significant, however, that the 'toffs' – that is, the Auxiliaries and the various underground intelligence networks – were not subject to sanction for their activities; whereas the Tans, being primarily of working-class origin, were from time to time arrested and subject to court-martial, albeit with limited results.

Winston Churchill was largely responsible for the creation of both the Auxiliaries and the Black and Tans; and his protégé Hugh Tudor owed his position to Churchill's patronage. It is hardly surprising that Churchill saw little wrong with what was taking place in Ireland: he viewed Ireland in the moral light of his father Randolph, who averred that no matter what the law, or Parliament, might have to say on the matter, it was the case that 'Ulster would fight and Ulster would be right'. In addition, Winston Churchill had an almost schoolboyishly naïve belief in the efficacy of what we might today call James Bond-like undercover activities. Prior to the arrival of the Tans in Ireland, his favourite prescription for curbing the activities of the IRA and the assassinations of the Squad in particular was a liberal application of the hangman's rope. Given such a moral and ideological context, then, Churchill's attitudes to the developing situation in Ireland seem clear: the fact that two hundred unarmed people were killed by crown forces in 1920 was a consequence of Sinn Féin activities, pure and simple.

The prevalence in 1920 – that 'Year of Terror' in Ireland – of legally sanctioned killings was made possible by the existence of two measures in particular. One was the introduction of martial law in Dublin, Cork and Tipperary in the spring of the year, followed in August by the introduction of the Restoration of Order in Ireland Act. The latter allowed for: 'The rigorous application of force by means of courts martial, the suspension of civil government, the stoppage of trains and motors, the withholdings of pensions and generally the infliction of a rapidly increasing paralysis in the country or an immediate attempt to conclude a pact with the leaders of Sinn Féin and the revolutionaries.' Considerably more energy, however, went into the 'rigorous application of force' than into the conclusion of any 'pact' – although underground peace feelers, conducted through such figures as Alfred Cope and Patrick Moylett (a London-based Irish businessman and associate of Lloyd George), flickered throughout the year. Such rigorous applications of force took various guises, none of them pleasant. Homes and businesses were burned, and indiscriminate reprisals and shootings occurred all over the country. The dead civilians included women and children. At Bantry in County Cork, a disabled boy was shot by chagrined Tans who missed finding his father on a raid. In Kiltartan in County Galway, a woman holding a child in her arms was killed when a policeman took a potshot at her from a passing lorry. Priests were amongst the targets: one, a Canon Thomas Magner of Dunmanway in County Cork, was shot for failing to toll his bell on Armistice Day.

The treatment meted out to Volunteers, however, tended to be even worse than that extended to civilians. The story of the group of Volunteers captured by Tans near Kerry Pike in County Cork passed into legend because of the condition of the bodies when they were recovered by their relatives; they could only be identified by their clothes. Following an IRA raid at Ballyduff in County Kerry which resulted in police deaths, the Tans arrived at the home of the Houlihan family at around

4am: they dragged the teenaged John Houlihan out of the house, and bayonetted and shot him, before crushing his skull with a rifle butt in front of his parents.

Such activities were not confined only to the ranks of Auxiliaries and Tans – for some significant names in British military history are also not kindly remembered in Ireland. 'Monty' – later Field Marshal Bernard Montgomery, with family connections in County Donegal – was one such. After serving in Ireland as an intelligence officer, he wrote in his memoirs: 'My own view is that to win a war of this sort you must be ruthless.' This belief, translated into action, caused him to be remembered in Cork as a nasty piece of work, albeit not a particularly successful one. Another significant military figure of the time was Arthur Percival, later best known as the leading British general in Singapore, and the man who ignominiously surrendered the colony to the Japanese in 1941. He is remembered in Ireland for presiding over torture, and enlivening his time in Cork by burning homes and taking potshots at farm workers in fields as he drove by; a favourite sideline was inserting splinters under the fingernails of his victims. He was a principal mover in the reprisal campaign, and ordered – for example – the burning of several homes and villages in the Cork area following a spate of IRA attacks, Michael Collins's old home at Woodfield being the best known of these properties.

Crow Street made a determined effort to kill Percival in England, after learning that he had gone there on holiday; he (wisely) stayed in a military barracks on that occasion, however, and proved impossible to reach. Then on 16 March 1921, it was learned that Percival would be arriving at Liverpool Street station in London at 3pm that very day. Thornton took a hand-picked unit including Pa Murray and Tadhg O'Sullivan to the station and waited for Percival's train to arrive. To Thornton's astonishment, Sam Maguire – the head of the IRB in London and a man who never broke cover if he could help it – turned up at the station too, shortly after the assassination squad had taken up its position. Maguire had just been given a tip-off that the police had been alerted to the ambush, and were at that very moment on their way to the station.

The Squad immediately vacated the station and a few minutes later a police cordon was thrown around the area. Passengers were held up and searched: in some cases they were detained for hours. Most of the unit remained in England for other operations: but Thornton succeeded in getting O'Sullivan aboard a coal boat bound for Cork. The passage was arranged courtesy of two IRB men, Steve Lanigan and Niall Kerr, who between them were largely responsible for the smuggling ring that brought arms and personnel in and out of Britain and sometimes (as in the case of de Valera) to America. Thornton stayed on in England a few days, and was duly smuggled back to Dublin on another coal boat. As he walked up O'Connell Street several days later, he bought the *Evening Herald* – and discovered that Tadhg O'Sullivan had been shot dead in Cork by a raiding party led by Percival.

Another prominent torturer who slipped the Squad net was Captain Jocelyn Lee Hardy, known to the IRA as 'Hoppy Hardy'. He was a particularly brave man: he had lost a leg in the Great War and was renowned for his attempts at escaping from German prisoner-of-war camps. But his activities in the intelligence room at Dublin Castle (known to the Squad as the 'knocking shop', because of the number of IRA men who had had their teeth kicked in there) had given him a rather different reputation in the eyes of Crow Street. As a result, Hardy seldom left the Castle except under heavy escort. Just the same, determined efforts were made to kill him: his would have been a prize scalp – but it was not to be. Hardy continued his career as interrogator and knocker of teeth, before retiring to a profitable new life in England as a novelist. Liam Tobin was interested in his work – but not impressed, and even in peacetime sent him anonymous death threats.

The most notable figure to serve in Ireland, however, was Sir Ormonde de l'Épée Winter, who arrived in Ireland in May 1920. Described by the British civil servant Mark Sturgis as looking like 'an amoral little white snake', as a young man, the then Captain Winter had been lucky to escape a murder charge after he killed a boy who had thrown stones at his boat with a blow of an oar to his head. The task of this gentleman was to establish a secret service organisation to plug the gap in the British intelligence operations caused by Collins's onslaught on the G-men. In response he is said to have been the moving spirit behind the setting up of both the Cairo and the Igoe gangs. Collins came to regard Winter as the most considerable of his British adversaries in Ireland, not least because he understood, as did Collins himself, the need for a reorganised structure that would serve and support the range of strategies deployed against the IRA. Such strategies, of course, took in everything from sophisticated counter-intelligence to bribery and torture, to the use of bloodhounds and secret addresses in Britain to which information about the IRA could be sent. Whatever Winter got up to, it was enough to cause his papers (held in the Public Record Office in London) to be sealed until the middle of the twenty-first century – as I discovered in the 1980s when I was researching my Michael Collins biography; this draconian embargo has, however, since been relaxed. Collins rated Winter sufficiently highly as to repeatedly try to kill him – though here too, the Squad never succeeded in claiming this highly prized scalp. Winter later became a successful horse breeder, and a convinced fascist who fought with the Finnish fascists against the Soviet Union at the outbreak of the Second World War.

One of Winter's greatest coups against Collins was the 1920 New Year's eve document raid on Eileen McGrane's flat in central Dublin which – as I mentioned earlier – fingered Ned Broy. In fact, Winter organised more than six thousand raids during his time in Ireland: a man of Collins-esque energy, he liked personally to see the raiding parties on their way from the Castle in the small hours of the morning – and then remain until they came back so that he could take part in the debrief. Winter, then, was a considerable and insightful opponent – and yet the fact remains that he, like so many of his colleagues in the service of the crown, failed to make much of a dent in Collins's highly burnished armour. For all the blood that was shed and lethal violence that was unleashed, Collins and his Apostles always slipped away.

Here it should be noted that the activities of Collins and the Squad were not always steeped in blood. Violence usually followed in their footsteps, it is true – but they were also involved in a number of daring escapades that have passed into legend. One of the most noteworthy was the attempt to free the Longford IRA leader John McKeon (better known in Ireland by the Irish version of his name, Seán Mac Eoin) from Mountjoy jail in Dublin. McKeon was a blacksmith by trade, and a chivalrous man by nature. On one occasion a police cordon was thrown around a cottage he was staying in: there were women in the house and, seeking to protect them, McKeon came out of the cottage with guns blazing, like a latter-day Ned Kelly (albeit without the armour). In this escapade, he managed to fatally wound an RIC officer, District Inspector McGrath, and escape. A month later, on 2 February 1921, McKeon ambushed a convoy of lorries containing RIC and Auxiliaries who were descending on Ballinalee to carry out a reprisal raid. After a gun battle lasting almost an hour, in which two Auxiliaries and a District Inspector of the RIC were killed, the fifteen members of the raiding party surrendered. Eight of them were wounded and, after disarming the party, McKeon directed that the captured men be given one of the lorries so that they could both effect an escape and drive the wounded to hospital.

A month later, McKeon himself was captured and handcuffed. He attempted to escape, but was shot and wounded and then beaten with rifle butts. Collins now decided that at all costs the blacksmith of Ballinalee should be rescued. With his facility for piecing disparate pieces of intelligence together, Collins made use of a piece of information from a Volunteer named Michael Lynch, who was on the run at the time. Previously, Lynch had been in charge of an abattoir run by Dublin Corporation at an address on North Circular Road – and now, Lynch told Collins that every morning, at six o'clock, an armoured car escorted an army lorry collecting meat for the garrison at Portobello barracks.

Charlie Dalton was instructed to attend a hastily convened meeting of the Squad. Collins himself was also present: and Dalton, who later recalled his awe at meeting Collins, was asked by Collins to go to Lynch's house, which overlooked the abattoir, and study the activities of the crew of the armoured car to see if there was any possibility of capturing it. In his subsequent statement, Dalton recalled that Lynch's wife showed him to his bedroom and that he looked out of the window to check for any possible escape route in the aftermath of the prospective ambush. It was a bright moonlit night – and this fact enabled Dalton to see to his horror that the abattoir was crawling with rats. He decided that he would prefer to be murdered in his bed rather than risk an escape which meant also escaping the rats.

The next morning Dalton was called in time by Mrs Lynch to witness the arrival of the armoured car through a blind on the bedroom window. Dalton saw the four-man crew of the armoured car leave the vehicle in order to have a cigarette: they then padlocked the door of the car so as to lock the remaining two members of the crew inside. This routine was followed for a week – after which Dalton was again summoned to a meeting

18. Death comes to Talbot Street: Dublin, 14 October 1920. A casualty is carried away following a gun battle in which Tipperary Volunteer Seán Treacy, two Auxiliaries and two civilians lost their lives.

19. Speaking to Irish America: Éamon de Valera addresses a meeting in Los Angeles during his US tour as President of Dáil Éireann.

20. The return of the chief: de Valera surrounded by supporters on his return to Ireland from the USA, December 1920.

21. A nation divided: George V inspects armed police during a visit to Ireland to open the Northern Ireland parliament, June 1921.

22. De Valera, Griffith and members of the Irish Delegation at their hotel in London, July 1921. Erskine Childers (second from the left in the back row), and Robert Barton (second from the right) would travel again to London for the Treaty negotiations proper in the autumn of 1921. De Valera's place would be taken by Collins – with momentous and tragic consequences.

23. History makers: left to right, Treaty negotiators George Gavan Duffy, Michael Collins, Arthur Griffith and Robert Barton; London, 11 October 1921.

24. Michael Collins and Gearóid O'Sullivan, right, at a ceremony marking the inauguration of the Irish Free State, Dublin, March 1922.

25. An anti-Treaty Convention at Dublin's Mansion House, 9 April 1922. Liam Lynch is fourth from left in the front row.

26. With civil war looming, armed anti-Treaty IRA men stalk a drizzly Grafton Street, July 1922.

27. Field Marshal Henry Wilson, Chief of the Imperial General Staff, was assassinated on his London doorstep on 22 June 1922 by two IRA Volunteers, almost certainly at Collins's behest.

28. Mourners at the funeral of Arthur Griffith, 16 August 1922. William T. Cosgrave, soon to be leader of the Irish Free State, is standing in the centre, glancing left. Behind him and on his left is the uniformed figure of Michael Collins, who himself has less than a week to live.

29. Last days: Michael Collins as Commander-in-Chief of the army of the Irish Free State, August 1922.

30. Free State soldiers at the funeral of Michael Collins, 28 August 1922. Liam Tobin and Tom Cullen are on the far left of the group.

31. General Richard Mulcahy, Collins's successor as army Commander-in-Chief, defeated the Republican side in the last months of the Civil War.

32. Commissioner of the Gardaí – and former double agent – Colonel
Eamon Broy receives counterfoils from a nurse during the Irish Hospitals
Sweepstake draw on the Cambridgeshire horse race, 28 October 1934.

with Collins. Dalton had made a sketch of the spot where the armoured car normally parked; and he also reported that on only one occasion during the week had the entire six-man crew left the armoured car. He told Collins that it could not be captured unless such an occasion repeated itself – and this in turn meant that some of the Squad would have to be on standby awaiting the right moment. The next stipulation was to ensure that one member of the Squad could drive the armoured car: a fearless Volunteer, Pat McCrae, who was a Squad driver, told the meeting that he would be able to drive the car – even though he had never driven an armoured vehicle before. Another difficulty was that the car had to be stolen silently – because if the alarm were raised, a nearby military barracks would be alerted. There were many potential issues – and yet Collins decided to go ahead with the plan to seize the car.

The bold objective was to use the vehicle to drive to Mountjoy, where two Volunteers dressed in British uniforms would then present themselves at the Governor's office demanding that McKeon be handed over to them, for transfer to Dublin Castle. For the plan to work, McKeon had to be in the Governor's office when the Squad party arrived: by that time the loss of the armoured car would have become known to the authorities and any delay would certainly have resulted in capture; and so it became necessary to get word to McKeon to fabricate some excuse to be taken to the Governor's office when the car arrived. It is clear that the entire scheme was already beyond foolhardy – and now Paddy Daly nearly succeeded in cranking the risk factor even beyond that! He had managed to get himself released from Ballykinler internment camp in County Down: it would appear that the authorities did not realise who Daly was – otherwise he would almost certainly have been executed rather than interned. Once interned, however, he risked the opprobrium of his fellow internees by 'signing out', reasoning correctly that he would be more use to the war effort outside the camp than in it. The 'signing-out' process involved convincing a tribunal that he would not take up arms if he was released. Since his wife had died recently, Daly promised that he would confine his activities to looking after his four children.

Amazingly, Daly's plea worked and a significant figure in the Squad was set free. Learning of the planned McKeon escape, Daly volunteered to take part in the mission. But two sympathetic warders from Mountjoy – who attended a briefing session Collins convened in Kirwan's pub – pointed out that Daly was well known to the prison Governor as a result of earlier Mountjoy sojourns. It was now decided that Joe Leonard would go in Daly's stead. A warder commented that Leonard would have 'some chance, as it was nine months since he was in Mountjoy'.

The next stage in this Mission Impossible was to get word to McKeon to somehow talk his way into the Governor's office at ten o'clock every morning for the foreseeable future, until the armoured car at the abattoir could be hijacked. By way of further encouragement, McKeon was instructed to delay the interviews as much as possible – and in addition to try to spend plenty of time in the corridor outside the Governor's office.

After word was sent to McKeon, the entire Squad was aug-mented by an active service unit of the Dublin Brigade of the IRA – and now, on 13 May 1921, the plan swung into opera-tion. On that first day, the armoured car could not be seized – but on the following morning, the soldiers, amazingly, left the vehicle: Dalton seized the opportunity and, dashing into the signal room, raised the blind. The awaiting Squad members immediately rushed into the abattoir yard, held up the soldiers, seized the padlock key from one of them, and rapidly changed into soldiers' uniforms themselves. In the course of this first phase of the operation, a Squad revolver went off – and one of the four soldiers inside the abattoir was shot dead as the others put up their hands.

Back in the house, Charlie Dalton locked Mrs Lynch and the children in a bedroom, to make it appear they had been held prisoners. He then rode his bicycle to a house on the North Circular Road where his brother Emmet and Leonard were waiting. Both were dressed as British officers: indeed, Emmet Dalton had in fact been one, having served with distinction at the Somme; and now he was wearing his old uniform, thus adding a note of verisimilitude to the adventure. 'Emmet', recalled Leonard, 'had all the appearance and manner of a British officer [...] he knew how to adopt the right tone in serving a Prisoner Removal on the jail authorities. I had served six months in Mountjoy and knew the prison well. Besides, Emmet's second uniform fitted me to perfection.'

Leaving the gasping Charlie Dalton to recover – his bicycle dash from the abattoir had left him rather breathless – the two 'officers' stepped out nonchalantly onto the footpath as the hijacked armoured car turned the corner. In it were Tom Keogh, Bill Stapleton and Jack Cafferty. Charlie Dalton again set off on his bicycle – this time to another Collins address in Middle Abbey Street to report of the progress of the operation so far. Collins commented, 'I hope the second part will be as successful.' However, the operation would prove to be something of a curate's egg – good only in parts.

The armoured car made its way to and into Mountjoy without difficulty, while some of the Squad at the abattoir remained to guard the imprisoned soldiers. At Mountjoy, Emmet Dalton – sitting outside the car as the officer normally did – waved an official-looking paper at the warder on lookout duty; and a set of three iron prison gates opened and shut behind the car. When they passed through the third gate, the driver – McCrea – manoeuvred the car into a position that prevented the gate being closed again. Leonard described what happened next. '[Emmet] Dalton and myself jumped smartly out of the car, we posted Tom Keogh, dressed in British dungarees and a Tommy's uniform cap, outside the main entrance door to cover our rear or give the alarm if necessary. Dalton and I entered the main door at 10.30am as the warders were coming from their quarter on duty. One of them, Warder Kelly, had known me as a prisoner...'

The warder in question had heard of prisoners doing well after they left prison – but not, perhaps, metamorphosing into British officers after nine months of liberty. Leonard's description continued, 'Warder Kelly was so surprised at seeing me in British uniform that he said; "Oh cripes, look at Leonard!" – and then clapping his hand over his mouth, dashed back upstairs.' One would have thought that this sighting would have ended the rescue attempt once and for all – but, with remarkable coolness, Dalton and Leonard continued on to the office of prison Governor Charles Monroe.

When they reached the office, they found it filled with warders – but there was no sign of McKeon; apparently these were new warders receiving a briefing, and while it was in progress McKeon was denied his visit to the Governor's office. Worse was to befall: the Governor apparently recognised Leonard and reached for the telephone to contact Dublin Castle to have the removal order verified. Leonard recalled, 'I sprang for the telephone and smashed it, while Dalton holding his gun held the staff at bay and then began tying the staff up in hope of finding the master keys.' While this was going on, meanwhile, Daly arrived on his bicycle fresh from the abattoir raid to join a group of Squad members. Now, they forced their way into the jail via a wicket gate which had been opened to allow a woman, Annie Malone, to hand in a parcel for one of the prisoners. Once the wicker gate entrance was secured, the Squad led by Sean Doyle held up the warders and opened the main gate; a sentry wounded one of the raiding party, Jack Walsh, in the hand with a lucky ricochet – but was highly unlucky himself when a shot from Tom Keogh killed him, causing the rifle to fall to the ground. Reasonably enough, Emmet Dalton and Leonard now concluded the shooting, signalled an end to their charade and headed for the armoured car. En route, Leonard again showed remarkable coolness and courage: spotting the rifle belonging to the sentry Keogh had shot lying on the ground and 'acting the part of a British officer', he barked out a series of orders both to a group of Auxiliaries on the prison roof and soldiers on the ground to withdraw. He recalled: 'On their refusal to obey, I took up the rifle knelt down and threatened to fire. The soldiers, seeing an officer kneeling in a firing position, retired to their quarters.' Leonard then jumped into the car and told McCrea to 'let her rip'.

With remarkable understatement, Leonard then described the 'ripping' process. 'Pat McCrea drove down that drive and onto the North Circular Road at a speed that was very satisfactory seeing that we were under rather heavy fire from the Prison.' Dalton and Leonard got safely to a waiting taxi and were driven to Howth. Here they found themselves 'dressed up as British officers, with no place to go'. Leonard's sister had friends in the Sisters of Charity – so they headed on the spur of the moment to a nearby convent where they were treated to 'a lovely cup of tea and the best china'. They were also treated to two new suits purchased from a nearby shop by the nuns. They exchanged these for their officers' uniforms and took the train back to Dublin.

The visit to the convent had been a flash of sudden inspiration on Leonard's part but, by way of indicating the intense planning and nerve-wracking waiting that went into most Squad operations, it should be noted that Joe Hyland, the owner of the taxi that had driven them to Howth, had waited at the pick-up spot for a number of nerve-wracking mornings previously, until Collins had sent word to him 'that there was nothing doing for that day'. Hyland later recalled that 'after a considerable delay, I saw an armoured car approaching me; by the way it was travelling with steam issuing from the engine, I sensed that it was our men!' Hyland then drove Dalton and Leonard to safety, and went back to trying to pick up fares.

Later that afternoon McCrea – who worked in a shop owned by his brother who supplied provisions to Portobello barracks – made a delivery to the barracks. He found the soldiers in a high state of readiness and asked a sergeant what was going on. The officer whispered his answer, 'Tell no-one, but the blinking Sinn Féiners are after stealing an armoured car!' McCrea responded by laughing and saying he didn't believe it – but the officer insisted that he was telling the truth; and that as far as he was concerned, the 'Shinners could be around the city shooting all before them.' All the other armoured cars around Dublin were recalled to barracks, and an aircraft was deployed to search for the missing car. McCrea's chuckling stopped, however, when he realised that he had left his collar in the armoured car. If it wasn't burnt, he could be identified from the laundry number. Daly sent a team around to the laundry to commandeer a customer list, and to warn the Scottish owner that he would be shot if he gave the name and address of any customer to the authorities.

The day after the Mountjoy raid, Collins wrote to the adjutant of the Longford Brigade saying that 'the men worked glorious and gallantly, but they just failed to achieve complete triumph, it was nobody's fault. There were no mistakes made.

Things went on splendidly till the last moment and then there was a mishap. Our men fought their way out of the prison and sustained only one slight casualty.' This was a reasonable assessment, provided one overlooks the small detail of Leonard having recently been a prisoner in the jail. It is the case, however, that Dalton, Leonard and the others took an incredible risk and showed courage of a high order. As for McKeon: he was eventually released under the terms of the truce of July 1921 – though only after Collins defiantly exceeded his authority and issued a public statement saying that there would be no truce until McKeon was freed.

This, then, was a courageous escapade – but it was an escapade just the same. It shows the lengths to which the Squad was prepared to go to protect their comrades – but it was by no means characteristic of what we will now see was a brutal and bloody war.

CHAPTER EIGHT

Bloody Sunday

The infamous Cairo Gang, a group of British Intelligence operatives active in Dublin during the War of Independence. Several of these men were killed on 'Bloody Sunday', 21 November 1920, in an operation planned by Michael Collins.

A S THAT DREADFUL YEAR OF 1920 WORE ON, SO EVENTS IN
Ireland became ever more harrowing. October saw the
death of Seán Treacy, who with Dan Breen had fired the first
shot in the war at Soloheadbeg. The two, as we have seen, had
been attached to the Squad by Collins, both because of their
deadly expertise and because their activities had made their
native Tipperary unsafe for them. Being on the run in unfamiliar
Dublin, the two men lived on short commons and found shelter
where they could. One such home was that of Professor John
Carolan in Drumcondra in north Dublin. This hiding place,
however, became known and the house was raided in the early
hours of 20 October. One of the leading members of the raiding
party was Major Gerald Smyth: he had been seconded from his
army posting in the Middle East to join the RIC, so that he
could avenge the death of his brother Bruce Smyth, killed at
Cork following his address to mutinous RIC officers at Listowel.

As the Drumcondra operation began, members of the raiding
party unwisely announced their presence by calling out for
Breen and Treacy to show themselves. Breen instead replied by
shooting and killing Smyth and another RIC inspector, while
Treacy escaped out of their bedroom window. Breen suffered
seven bullet wounds but managed to wound another RIC man

before also escaping through the bedroom window and running along a roof until he managed to find a skylight and drop down. Incredibly, he managed to shoot his way through a police cordon and somehow make his way to a sympathiser's home – a procedure which involved completing a distance of several miles while suffering from severe blood loss. At his refuge, Dick McKee was alerted and came with a car to bring Breen to the Mater Hospital, where he was treated under an alias.

Treacy now made a decision that proved to be fatal for him. He had a formidable reputation: I remember as a boy comic-book stories describing the strange arrangement of buttons he sported on his coat and waistcoat that supposedly enabled him to draw and fire faster than any Wild West gunman. But despite such myths, Treacy was in fact a sensitive person who once rebuked Collins for cursing in front of a woman, and who did not take to killing lightly. He had deliberately advocated the shooting of the two RIC men at Soloheadbeg and would have in fact preferred to have shot six policemen, according to Breen, because the deaths would have had a greater impact on public opinion, showing that the Volunteers meant business. Yet he always prayed for his victims, and he attended the funeral of the two inspectors who had been shot in the Carolan raid. Afterwards he headed for the 'Republican outfitters': Peadar Clancy's tailoring shop in Talbot Street. Unbeknownst to him, however, Collins had earlier organised the Squad to attack the inspectors' funeral in the belief that senior figures were planning to attend. When he discovered that they would not in fact be in attendance, Collins called off the attack.

Some of the most important Crow Street figures had gathered at Clancy's premises before the countermanding order arrived; these included Tobin, Cullen and McKee. The group scattered on receiving word from Collins – but, unaware of what had happened, Treacy cycled to the shop. This Tipperary man didn't like cities and, without Breen at his side, he felt exposed and vulnerable. He had intended to cycle back to Tipperary after visiting Clancy's but he was spotted arriving at the shop on his bicycle, and an effort was made to arrest him. An Auxiliary officer named Frank Christian held him up at gunpoint – and there must have been something in the comic-book's account of Treacy's quick-draw buttons: because, although he was held up by an armed and trained British officer, he still managed to draw and kill him. He also managed to grapple with another Auxiliary, who fired at him. But Treacy disarmed him and, now armed with two purloined Auxiliary weapons, attempted to engage a lorryload of soldiers. The soldiers replied with a fusillade of rifle bullets that killed Treacy, the Auxiliary and two innocent civilians.

Another death was to follow some days later, that of Professor Carolan – but not before he had made a statement describing how, after Breen and Treacy had escaped, he himself was put up against a wall and shot, lingering for some days from the wound. Breen himself recovered from his injuries, the nuns and nurses at the Mater Hospital seeing to it that he was pushed into hiding places when raiding parties descended on the hospital. (Collins, who had a particular admiration for fighting men, turned up himself on occasion when he heard a raid was in progress, watching anxiously until the raiders departed.)

As is often the case, Breen seems to have been more appreciated abroad than he was in Ireland itself: in the eyes of one historian, Michael T. Foy, he was 'brutally unappealing and thick skinned'. However, I interviewed him towards the end of his life: and found him humorous, knowledgeable and still full of his own particular brand of irreverent courage. Still atheistic, he told me about how a fellow inmate in his nursing home had been pressuring him to return to the Church. 'I told him', said Breen, 'that whichever of us died first would come back and tell the other one whether there was a God or not. Well, the bastard has been dead now for several weeks and he hasn't been back yet!' Breen achieved international recognition with his book *My Fight for Irish Freedom*, which became a bible for some Indian Nationalists. Inspired by Breen, they staged a 1916-esque Easter Rising in the Punjab in 1930. The centrepiece of their onslaught was to be the European club where British officers and administrators congregated – but they had reckoned without the effect of the Christian festival; the club was shut for Good Friday. As in Dublin in 1916, some sixteen insurgents were earmarked for execution. But it was their luck that the top British official in the region was Sir John Anderson who had also been the top British civil servant in Dublin Castle during the Irish war of independence. Mindful of the effect of the 1916 executions he saw to it that no one was shot or hanged – until, that is, about three years later, when the leader of this Punjab Rising was eventually caught and executed.

October also witnessed the death, after a long period of suffering, of Terence Mac Swiney. He had been on hunger strike for seventy-four days inside Brixton prison in south London, in protest at his internment and trial by a military court. IRA volunteer Joseph Murphy died on the same day (25 October), but Mac Swiney's status as MP and Lord Mayor of Cork ensured that his plight and death attracted worldwide media attention. Back in Ireland, eleven other prisoners in Cork jail were also on hunger strike – but now Arthur Griffith ordered that their protest cease; Mac Swiney's death, it was hoped, would suffice. The hunger strikes illustrated the survival of one notable aspect of the Irish tradition of physical force: a willingness to endure, as well as to inflict, suffering. Mac Swiney's death transformed the nomenclature of the struggle into one of martyrdom. At first, Collins hoped to turn the funeral cortège into a vast media event, by having it move slowly through Britain and across the sea to Dublin, before travelling onward to Cork. This aspect, at least, was stymied by British officials, who ordered that the coffin be shipped directly from England to Cork.

The fires, however, had been lit – and they were fanned days later, on 1 November, when the teenager Kevin Barry was hanged in Dublin for his part in a raid on a bakery. His execution – on the Catholic feast of All Saints – also attracted worldwide attention: but the British held firm, arguing that Barry's youth could not protect him; after all, teenaged British soldiers had also been shot during the bakery raid. Barry's execution, however – to say nothing of the reports which circulated, alleging ill-treatment in prison – gave rise to a ballad that is still sung in Ireland today. The young Barry was eulogised as being: 'Another martyr for old Ireland / Another murder for the crown.'

It may be, however, that the ballad need never have been written had Barry's family acceded to Collins's wishes. There seems to have been a breakdown in communication at this point between Collins and the bulk of the Squad. Two Squad members, Bernard Byrne and Jimmy Conroy, were within seconds of attempting a rescue of Barry, when his sister Eileen told Byrne that if the attempt went ahead, she would make a public scene – for she, like the rest of the Barry family believed that the prisoner was about to be reprieved. Even by the standards of the Squad, the proposed rescue plan was extraordinarily daring. Byrne was to take care of two Auxiliaries who guarded the visiting room; Conroy, meanwhile, was to deal with the guard at the gate. In the preceding days Byrne and other Volunteers had visited the prison, familiarising themselves with layouts and routines: they had established that the guard changed at 4pm; and so the rescue attempt was timed for not later than 3.45pm, in the expectation that the guard would be relaxed, and reflexes slow. It had been arranged that a priest would visit Barry shortly after 3pm and that Eileen Barry's visit would almost overlap with that of the priest, so that they would still be in the Governor's office when Byrne and Conroy struck.

When Eileen Barry arrived at the prison, however, she told Conroy that the family had information that Barry was going to be reprieved during the coming weekend, that she would therefore take no part in the proposed rescue – and that she would cause a scene if the rescue was not aborted. Byrne remembers with masterly understatement that 'This left me in a somewhat awkward position' – for Kevin Barry himself, who was aware of the planned rescue, by that stage should have been running down the prison corridor in the direction of the main gate where, hopefully, Conroy would have kept the warders at bay. Byrne told Eileen Barry that he and the others were prepared to go ahead with the rescue – but that if she were considering interfering rather than facilitating the rescue, he had to consider his responsibility towards the other men involved: Kevin was her brother, but both inside and outside the jail by this time there were some ten other Volunteers to consider. In the event no agreement was forthcoming – and Byrne and Conroy just managed to exit the prison as the relief guard arrived.

One of the most extraordinary features of this very detailed account by one of the most reliable and experienced members of the Squad is that it is almost completely contradicted by another account from Oscar Traynor, who was one of the most reliable men in the entire independence movement. Traynor recalled that he and Peadar Clancy were ordered to dress as clergymen and go to Mountjoy, enter the visiting room where they would hold up the guards, remove Barry and make their way to the gate where another party of Volunteers would have held up the guards – and thus would they make their escape. A final meeting on the implementation of this plan was held on the Sunday morning before Barry's execution – and word was sent to his mother, who was expected to visit the jail that day. However, Traynor – who was sitting in a room in the house where the meeting was taking place – was informed by the Brigade OC Dick McKee that Mrs Barry was very upset at the prospect of possibly more lives being lost; and in the absence of any positive guarantee that the attempt would succeed she did not want any rescue attempt made. Traynor did not hear what the courier who brought this message to McKee actually said. But thirty years later, he was able to recall the enormous relief he felt when the attempt was called off. Just who was supposed to go into the prison and the exact details of the planned escape will always, then, be subject for debate. But it is quite clear that the Barry family opposed the attempt. Kevin Barry was hanged the following Monday.

The Barry execution affected Michael Collins deeply. Observers have left accounts of their leader throwing down his pen from time to time and groaning 'poor Barry'. As though to compound the effect of his execution, moreover, the British made the mistake of selecting the feast of All Saints (1 November) for the hanging: the British official Mark Sturgis remarked in his diary that it was 'rather a pity no one noticed it is All Saints' Day'. As a result of Barry's execution, reprisal attacks on crown forces were ordered by Collins. This instruction, however, was subsequently countermanded – most likely because, as with the death of Mac Swiney, the publicity for martyrdom paid considerably more dividends than that for killings. Yet the countermanding order does not appear to have reached the organising committee of the County Kerry Brigade of the IRA. Instead, all hell broke loose in the Kingdom: and in the aftermath of Barry's execution, seven policemen were shot dead, nine were wounded, and two were kidnapped. Although these last were later released, they were so brutally treated in captivity that one of them later committed suicide. There was a massive British reaction to this swelling of violence – a reaction that was totally counterproductive in terms of winning hearts and minds.

Black and Tan atrocities were inevitably widespread – but the town of Tralee bore the brunt of these operations. Two RIC constables attacked by the IRA in the onslaught following Kevin Barry's death are known to have been shot – and then a rumour went around that they had been thrown into the furnace of the local Tralee gasworks, enraging the Black and Tans still further. In fact, they had been shot and their bodies dumped in thick mud at a spot where a canal empties into Tralee Bay. This, as it turned out, was a bad place to dispose of corpses: for, whether through the action of the sea or the scouring properties of the canal, the mud did not hold the bodies. It was a grisly scene: for some time afterwards the lock-keeper had the disagreeable task of informing the IRA gloomily that 'they [the bodies] came up again' – and the IRA had the equally unpleasant task of pushing the bodies back under the mud until they eventually disintegrated.

The onslaught on Tralee in November 1920 lasted for almost two weeks, and rapidly gained international attention. The Tans took to driving around in their lorries, firing indiscriminately. On All Saints' Day, they fired on the congregation as it emerged from noon mass at St John's church: there was mass panic – and this mass panic was recorded by the international media corps which had gathered in this corner of Ireland to attend the Mac Swiney funeral in nearby Cork. One of these journalists was the Englishman Hugh Martin of the *Daily News*, whom the Tans' leadership regarded as being unduly sympathetic to the natives. Martin had what the Tans considered to be a bad habit of making comparisons between ruined towns and villages in Ireland and the horrors he had seen in Belgium during the Great War. Now, a group of Tans who were briefing the visiting press corps made the mistake of telling the journalists that Martin was on their hit list. This snippet of information made news around the world: and even the London *Times* carried a leading article condemning the threat in Ireland to press freedom.

The Tans also insisted that the funerals of their comrades called for as much respect as did that of, for example, Mac Swiney – with the result that they ordered that all business premises be closed down at such times. The result was described by the London correspondent of *Le Journal*:

I do not remember, even during the war, having seen a people so profoundly terrified as those of the little town of Tralee. The violence of the reprisals undertaken by representatives of authority so to speak, everywhere has made everybody beside himself, even before facts justify such a state of mind. [...] The town was as deserted and doleful as if the Angel of Death had passed through it [...] All the shops shut [...] all work was suspended, even the local newspapers.

Indeed, the town was shut fast: schools were closed, and nothing moved in the streets except for the crown forces which fired at windows and shops as they drove up and down. The sense of panic was heightened when, after a few days of this indiscriminate shooting, the Black and Tans began to systematically firebomb businesses owned by Sinn Féin sympathisers. The *Cork Examiner* reported 'the screams of the women and children were heard from the neighbourhood of the burning buildings, mingled with the ring of rifle fire and the explosion of bombs'.

In the House of Commons, Sir Hamar Greenwood announced that enquiries would be held into some of the cases of fatal shootings – although he rather undermined public confidence in the integrity of such investigations (assuming that Irish public opinion had ever believed in such integrity in the first place) by telling the House that one of the Irish dead 'bore no traces of gunshot or other wounds'. The London *Times* reporter had, in sharp contrast, already written that he had seen a bullet wound in a dead man's head. Other press reports stated that the British army commander in the area was trying to protect the citizens from the police (that is, the Tans) – but that he was doing so without authority as the law provided the Tans with full protection.

It was indeed the case, in Tralee as elsewhere in Ireland, that the regular army did attempt to maintain a more humane attitude and better discipline than did the Tans, the Auxiliaries or the unacknowledged death squads which formed part of the intelligence effort. The Prime Minister, however, made it clear which set of military attitudes *he* preferred. On 9 November 1920, Lloyd George made a famous speech at Guildhall in the City of London, in which he said that the government had grasped 'murder by the throat'. In Ireland, this was generally taken to mean Kevin Barry's throat in particular – but in Tralee the Prime Minister's words had a particularly numbing effect. The 9th of November was the first day since the feast of All Saints that the town had attempted to restore some semblance of normality. That is, shops were open – although Tans stood outside bakeries, butchers and any stores selling food, threatening would-be shoppers with bayonets and firing shots if they tried to enter. By now, however, the townsfolk were hungry: the media reported that there had been no work in town for a week: this meant no wages to buy food – and all in a context in which shops had been in any case forced to close. In faraway Montreal, the *Gazette* reported that:

> Black and Tans take up position outside bakeries and provision stores where they suspect food could be secured, and at the bayonet point send famishing women and children from the doors. Outside one baker's establishment a Black and Tan brandishing a revolver told women and children to clear off adding 'you wanted to starve us, but we will starve you'.

The threat of hunger, moreover, was particularly resonant in an area which had suffered greatly during the Famine and in which folk memories of that catastrophe remained all too vivid.

Sir Hamar's response to the situation in Tralee, including the commercial chaos in the town, was to inform the House that the shops had been closed following the assassinations of policemen, that the closures were not ordered by the police, that he understood that the shops were now opening, and that he was awaiting the result of an inquiry into who had given the order for the shops to be closed. A perusal of the *New York World*, however, might have assisted Sir Hamar's efforts to find out who had closed the shops: 'Black and Tan rule has been set up in Tralee. Many of the 10,000 inhabitants have fled, but those unable to find refuge elsewhere are the victims of this awful procedure.'

On the surface, then, it may have appeared as though the British military at this time was asserting its tight grasp on Ireland. By mid-November, however, it was clear that this was not so – and that beneath the surface, Collins and his operation remained as potent as ever. A scene would be played out on a single day, on the streets and playing fields of Dublin, that encapsulated the bitter hatreds and fears of this period in Irish history, and that demonstrated to every participant and observer that an endgame was now underway. That day became known as Bloody Sunday. For Collins and his Apostles, indeed, the endgame was already upon them. Although their intelligence resources remained second to none, it was now time to assert themselves over the British in this regard – for once and for all.

At this point in November 1920, a number of British military officers were living under cover at different addresses around

Dublin – from where they issued forth by night to organise raids which ended, as often as not, in both arrests and executions. As I have mentioned previously, the wife of one of these officers, Caroline Woodcock, is an improbably useful source of information about these fraught days: for she left a picture of the raids as told to her by her husband and his colleagues:

If the house was moderately clean this work was bearable but unpleasant. Some of the descriptions [...] of some of the filthy tenement houses in which Dublin's slums abound made me quite ill. A dozen people in a room and five or six in a bed was quite usual: imagine searching such a bed and pulling the mattresses to pieces. One officer told me that he had found four human beings, two ducks and a lamb in one bed – not to speak of smaller and unmentionable animals. A few days in hospital subsequent to a raid such as this to get rid of a complaint common amongst the great unwashed was often necessary.

Woodcock did, however, concede that other types of raids, involving the sealing of streets and multiple arrests, were rather more important – and she went on to describe how the raiders themselves were subjected to searches upon their return to barracks, because of the 'whines and complaints, totally unjustifiable, of the Irish rebels who invariably claimed compensation from the hated British government for articles missing from their houses after a raid – articles which they had probably never possessed'. Woodcock also particularly objected to the fact that the guidelines as to how the soldiers should conduct themselves during raids called for the adoption of 'a courteous but firm attitude toward the inhabitants of a raided house'. Woodcock commented that 'truly, we are a nation of fools even if gentlemen'.

Collins was doubtless not so much concerned with courtesy or the lack of it during house searches. Instead, what worried him was a third form of raid, described in Caroline Woodcock's inimitable, sanitised manner:

> There is yet a third sort of raid, which is undertaken by two or three daring spirits only [...] desperate and much-wanted members of the IRA are always surrounded by their own particular guards and spies [...] the only chance of getting them is a sudden dash [...] the raiders know well that shooting is bound to come, and it is just a question of who gets a shot in first. These raids usually end in tragedy.

These raids did indeed end in tragedy – but episodes such as the shooting of John Lynch in Dublin's Exchange Hotel on the night of 23 September 1920 demonstrate what really occurred in the course of them. Lynch was in Dublin on financial business with Collins, and the latter subsequently discovered, as he wrote to Arthur Griffith:

> At 1.35am on the morning of the murder, phone message was received from Captain Baggelly, General Staff, Ship Street Barracks [...] to send a car. A car was sent [...]

members of the RIC force picked up a small party of military [...] and proceeded to the Royal Exchange Hotel. At 2.15am, a phone message passed from the headquarters of the Dublin district to College Street station, giving the information that the RIC had been to the Royal Exchange Hotel and shot a man named Lynch. There is not the slightest doubt that there was no intention whatever to arrest Mr Lynch.

Collins decided that the correct course of action was to assassinate the Captain Baggellys of this world, using information from Lily Mernin and a variety of other sources – such as the maids who cleaned their lodgings and the porters who guarded their doors. It would be done, moreover, in spectacular fashion: for, having secured the addresses of a number of officers staying at different addresses in the city, it was decided to assassinate them *en bloc* on the morning of Sunday 21 November 1920. The plan for these coordinated assassinations was drawn up by Frank Thornton, who had to explain and justify his plan before a joint meeting of both the Dáil cabinet and the Volunteers' Army Council. The justification of each name on the list was queried by Cathal Brugha: he gradually reduced the total number of personnel taking part in the operation, before giving it the green light.

On Saturday night, 20 November, Collins attended Dublin's Gaiety Theatre in the company of David Neligan and others. He wondered aloud about the type of men who were to be killed the next day: what sort, he wondered, were they? Neligan replied that all Collins had to do was look into the next theatre box – where he could see some of them for himself. This was a job in which the hunter and the hunted lived truly cheek by jowl. It was also, however, a job so large that it called for more resources than the Squad alone could provide – and so the killing machine had to be augmented by a number of other Volunteers, not all of whom could be considered suitable for such bloody work, and at least one of whom would suffer psychiatric problems for the rest of his life. Another Volunteer, incidentally, was a youthful Seán Lemass – who almost forty years later would become Irish Taoiseach.

Hours later, the operation began that would result in the deaths of up to nineteen British operatives – and once again Caroline Woodcock steps into the narrative. Here, she describes what happened to one of the officers, a Captain Brian Christopher Keenlyside of her husband's regiment. When the young raiders tried to kill him, 'He had been placed against a wall in the hall and a group of men took or tried to take careful aim at him. One man's hand shook so much that a comrade took his revolver away from him, and another supported his trembling left hand on his right arm.' Keenlyside was shot in the jaw and in both arms, but survived. Woodcock averred that 'like my husband, this man also was a regimental officer and had nothing to do with police or secret service'.

One of the most miraculous escapes of all, indeed, was that of Caroline Woodcock's husband, Lieutenant-Colonel Wilfred James Woodcock. He had attempted to go downstairs to warn some of his comrades that something was amiss – this, after his keen-eyed wife, who had been standing at a window, spotted a man getting over the garden wall and taking a revolver out of his pocket. Colonel Woodcock obviously belonged to the 'stiff upper lip' school of army behaviour: after shouting at his wife to keep watching at the window, he got shot himself and staggered back into the bedroom, telling her, 'It's alright darling, they have only hit outlying portions of me.' Woodcock, in fact, had been hit four times – but he subsequently recovered.

Others in the Woodcock quarters were not so lucky. A Lieutenant-Colonel Montgomery opened the door of his room, and Woodcock – who had been ordered to turn and face the wall – shouted at his colleague to 'Look out!' Montgomery was shot dead. Charlie Dalton and Paddy Flanagan, meanwhile, knocked at a door to a room in the top of the same house, and when it was opened by the occupant, a C. M. G. Dowling, they shot him dead. A Captain Leonard Price in the next room was fatally wounded. For a long time afterwards Dalton could not sleep, reliving as he did the sound of the dying officer's blood gurgling out onto the floor. The fact is that for some of the Volunteers involved in these mass raids, this was the first time they had taken life. Nerves, then, accounted for the miraculous escape of men like Keenlyside and Woodcock.

Sheer luck accounted for other escapes, such as those of a Major Callaghan and a Colonel Jennings who were to have spent the night in the Eastwood hotel, but instead apparently spent it in a brothel. Other officers, for whatever reason, had either moved lodgings or simply didn't come home on the night before the killers arrived. But other targets were not so lucky.

Vinnie Byrne left an account of the shooting of Lieutenant George Bennet and Peter Ames, after a maid had admitted him and his men to 38, Upper Mount Street in south Dublin. The maid – clearly a sympathiser – directed the assassins in the right direction, bedroom after bedroom: and acting on her advice, Byrne and two other Volunteers, Sean Doyle and Herbie Conroy, entered Bennet's room, where they found the officer in the act of reaching for a gun under his pillow. Doyle seized the revolver and told the officer to put his hands up; he was then directed into a back room, where he was joined by Ames. Byrne now silently urged the Lord to have mercy on the souls of both men – and shot them dead.

Other operations were rather less streamlined. Nearby, at 92 Lower Baggot Street, Captain W. F. Newbury was living with his wife in a flat. When a section of the Squad led by Joe Leonard and Bill Stapleton asked the housekeeper whether Newbury was at home, the woman replied that she didn't know – but the assassins clearly did, for they made straight for his bedroom door. They knocked, and his wife – who was in an advanced state of pregnancy – opened the door and then slammed it shut when she saw the men standing outside with revolvers in their hands. She and her husband made a break for another room, slamming that door also – but Newbury was shot through the door and then shot several more times as he tried to get out a window. His wife covered the body with a blanket. She lost the baby a week later.

One of the operations which miscarried because the target hadn't come home took place at 7 Ranelagh Road in south

Dublin, where a Captain Nobel and his girlfriend were the targets. In his description of what happened, Dan McDonnell said: 'We got a very ugly mission to perform [...] to kill a British agent called Nobel and his paramour. [...] they were both agents and our information was that they were both the main cause of a member of our organisation named Doyle getting a very cruel death in the Dublin mountains.' But when McDonnell and Joe Dolan burst into Nobel's room, 'We found the room empty, except for a half-naked woman; she did not scream or say a word,' recalled Todd Andrews, one of the Volunteers who had been drafted in to augment the Squad's numbers. The man they were looking for had apparently got up and gone on some assignment shortly after 7am. When a man came out of the next room, Andrews went to shoot him, assuming that he was Nobel. Just in time one of the raiding party called out, 'He's alright!' – for this man was actually the one who had supplied the Squad with their intelligence.

According to Andrews, Dolan and McDonnell then set about behaving like Black and Tans – even though the house contained only women and children: in their search for papers they overturned furniture, pushing occupants of the house around, and either through carelessness or malice set fire to a room in which there were children. Andrews continued that he felt shame and embarrassment at witnessing the plight of Nobel's mistress – but Dolan and McDonnell were not in a chivalrous mood. Their orders had been to shoot her if they found her together with Nobel, but not if she was alone. Dolan was so angry at missing Nobel that he described giving 'the poor girl a right

scourging with the sword scabbard. Then I set the place on fire.'
McDonnell and Dolan's behaviour outraged other Volunteers –
and one of them, Francis Coughlan, remained at the house to
see the children to safety, and to put out the flames.

Later that same day, a shocking reprisal took place. This
was the Croke Park massacre, which took place when a large
party of Auxiliaries and Black and Tans invaded the headquarters of the Gaelic Athletic Association as a match between
Dublin and Tipperary was taking place. The soldiers claimed
that they were fired on first – although no casualties were
reported. What is not disputed, however, is that the raiding
party opened up on the crowd with rifles and machine guns.
Fourteen people were shot dead – including the Tipperary
goalkeeper Michael Hogan, after whom Croke Park's famous
Hogan stand is named – and hundreds more were injured.

The death toll for Bloody Sunday did not end with the Croke
Park shootings. In a raid on the Saturday night, one of the
British undercover intelligence squads got lucky, and captured a
figure who after Collins was probably the most important IRA
commander in the country. This was Dick McKee, founder of
the IRA's Dublin Brigade, who along with Peadar Clancy and
Conor Clune, an Irish-language student who had nothing to
do with the Squad, were picked up in separate swoops. The
trio were tortured in Dublin Castle during the night of 20/21
November, and their bayonetted bodies were discovered the
following day. It was said that they had been shot 'while trying
to escape'. This story was so unlikely that amongst those who
doubted it (having visited the Castle room where they died)

was Sir John Anderson. Collins was devastated: 'We're finished now,' he said at first – but it soon became evident that McKee had died without talking. The Crow Street operation remained inviolate, and the Apostles were able to continue their work.

Collins, meanwhile, showed his courage to what could fairly be described as a crazy degree when the bodies of McKee and the others were handed back for burial. The faces were so badly marked that the clergy ordered that the coffins be closed. But Collins turned up at the church clad in his Volunteer uniform, oblivious to the spies and police in the vicinity, and insisted that the coffins be unsealed, and the corpses inside be dressed in their uniforms. The following day, and in the presence of an even bigger audience of Castle agents, he stood beside the graves as the burials took place. A photograph of him attending the funeral appeared in the early edition of the *Evening Herald* – but the Squad visited the offices of the paper and the photo was removed, never to appear again.

Very shortly afterwards, on 5 February 1921, the man who had betrayed McKee and the others was removed from the scene. This was John Ryan, a military policeman in Dublin Castle. Because of his position, he was able to roam the streets at night despite the curfew, and Crow Street became aware that he used this permission to track wanted IRA men. It was discovered that he had in fact placed a tell-tale chalk mark on the door of the house on Gloucester Street where McKee and Clancy were sleeping. Ryan's movements were tracked to Hynes' public house on the corner of Gloucester Place – and eight members of the Squad, led by Vinnie Byrne, were assigned to shoot him. There was a church near the pub where a funeral was in progress. One of the cab men outside the church called out to the Squad, 'Are you going to the funeral?' Tom Keogh replied: 'No, we're going to arrange one.' After checking out the other customers in the bar, the killers decided that the man they wanted was the one sitting at the counter reading a racing newspaper. But as they couldn't see his face because of the newspaper, Byrne asked him what was the tip for that day's 3.30 race? Ryan lowered the paper to reply, was recognised and, as Bernard C. Byrne recalls in his deposition to the Bureau of Military History, 'without any discussion or delay, Keogh fired on him, I doing likewise… Ryan would betray no more members of our organisation.'

What did Bloody Sunday achieve? As anyone who has had experience of terrorist events can testify, one of the most demoralising events of underground warfare is the receipt of a message from the other side saying: 'We know where you live.' Bloody Sunday made it unmistakably clear to the hosts of British agents in Dublin that they could never feel safe, by day or night, in the streets or in the ostensible peace of their own lodgings. Nobody, not even a revisionist historian, has attempted to dispute the fact that in the hours after the shoot-ings, all the houses, apartments and spare rooms in Dublin Castle were filled to overflowing, as a terrified horde of agents poured out of their supposedly safe houses into safer accom-modation; as Dave Neligan – who was on duty in the Castle at this time – noted, a bed could not be had within the Castle compound for love nor money.

As to the disputed death toll of nineteen: unquestionably, some personnel not connected with espionage were shot, through being in the wrong place at the wrong time. Frank Thornton, in his very comprehensive account of his Crow Street activities for the Bureau of Military History which he compiled several years after the event, places the number of dead officers at nineteen, rather than the fourteen of popular lore – but it is most likely the case that while nineteen officers were shot, some of them might not have been engaged in espionage. I will leave the last word to the redoubtable Caroline Woodcock – who subsequently described her amazement at finding out just what the undercover units had been doing. Woodcock admitted, 'I had seen these men leaving the house night after night, but I never knew or guessed what their work was.' Significantly, Woodcock became enlightened through talking to 'one of the *few survivors* of the original intelligence service'.

There were several ferocious postscripts to the events of that November night and day. A week later, on 27 November, the Apostles stretched out a hand to Britain itself: an undercover unit broke into the warehouses on the docks at Liverpool – at that time, one of Britain's most important ports – and set fire to fifteen of them, plus two timber yards; the resulting inferno stretched for four miles along the Mersey. Collins also suc-ceeded in securing the British addresses of a number of the Black and Tans serving in Ireland. Their homes were raided and burnt.

The day after the Liverpool fires, a major IRA operation occurred in Ireland at Kilmichael in County Cork. Here a unit of the Cork No. 3 Brigade, led by Tom Barry ambushed and killed a lorryload of Auxiliaries – some seventeen in all. In recent years this ambush became the centre of controversy, when the late Canadian historian Peter Hart alleged that Barry gave the order to fire on the survivors after they had surrendered their arms. But Hart's credibility was severely undermined when the Irish historian Meda Ryan revealed that the source of some of Hart's information was a man who had died *before* Hart claimed to have interviewed him. Indeed, I would suggest that Kilmichael, together with reassessments of both Bloody Sunday and Collins's overall achievements all became part of a debunking attempt on the part of some writers influenced by equal measures of colonial cringe, British and Unionist propaganda and some genuine public revulsion at the war in Northern Ireland. However, at the time – with Ireland suffering under the lash of the Auxiliaries and the Tans – Kilmichael was hailed as a significant victory. The event subsequently gave rise to a rebel ballad, *The Boys of Kilmichael*:

On the twenty-eighth day of November,
The Tans left the town of Macroom.
They were seated in Crossley tenders,
Which brought them right into their doom.
They were on the high road to Kilmichael,
And never expecting to stall.
'Twas there that the boys of the column
They made a clear sweep of them all.

CHAPTER NINE

De Valera Intervenes

The Custom House in Dublin burns after being captured and destroyed by the Dublin Brigade of the IRA, 25 May 1921.

TOWARDS THE END OF 1920, ÉAMON DE VALERA RETURNED from his long spell in the United States. It was a change that would have a direct bearing on the workings of the Squad, especially as it seems evident in hindsight that his return had much to do with the increasing power of Collins in Irish affairs, as with any other factor. The arrest of Arthur Griffith in December 1920 meant that Collins, in addition to his other roles, was now acting President of Sinn Féin – and this did not sit well with de Valera, who was monitoring continually the ebbs and flows of Irish affairs from afar.

The pair, even with the Atlantic between them, continued to have a testy relationship, with various spats playing out across the seas. They had always been very different types – and now the differences between them yawned wider than ever. Collins, of course, was living a life fraught with continual tension and violence – this in sharp contrast to de Valera, who was running his Irish publicity campaigns from the comfort of a plush suite at the Waldorf Astoria Hotel in Manhattan. Tension over the questions of financial bonds had been smoothed over; and now de Valera's imperious ways began to anger the powerful Irish-American lobby in America itself. The influential John Devoy had his revenge on de Valera by printing a large picture of Collins accompanying an admiring article in his powerful Irish-American newspaper under the banner heading: 'Ireland's fighting chief'. He also wrote an editorial saying 'Michael Collins speaks for Ireland'. Though Collins objected to the coverage, it marked an undeniable contrast between Collins's hunted existence in Ireland and de Valera's comfortable life in America.

Given this atmosphere of rancour in America and the growing strength of underground peace-feelers in Ireland, it was becoming evident to all that de Valera's time in America was now at an end. Collins organised for him to be smuggled back into Ireland in December 1920. The new year therefore opened with both leaders of Republican Ireland on the same island once again. De Valera was now preoccupied with two different forms of manoeuvring: one against the British, and the other against Collins. Indeed, practically his first remarks on arriving in Ireland indicated the tone which was to dominate: Collins had arranged that de Valera was to be met in Dublin by Tom Cullen and spirited to a safe house. De Valera asked Cullen how things were going – and Cullen replied, with more enthusiasm than diplomacy, that things were going great: sure, the Big Fellow was leading them and things were going splendidly. To which de Valera replied: 'Big Fellow! We'll see who's the Big Fellow' – and angrily struck the dockside rail with his fist.

De Valera, it must be remembered, had returned to Dublin trailing clouds of near-deification for what were regarded in Ireland as his achievements in the US. He had received tumultuous welcomes from Irish Americans everywhere he went.

Twenty-one-gun salutes were not uncommon, and venues like Chicago's Fenway Park were packed with Irish emigrants over-joyed at the opportunity of being able to hear and see the President of the Irish Republic – for so he allowed himself to be styled. He had gone to America as An Príomh Aire (the First Minister) – but the Irish-American leader Joseph McGarrity speedily convinced him that Americans would not be able to get their heads around An Príomh Aire. This was a Republic – and its citizens could relate to a leader of another nascent Republic who styled himself simply as President. Which was all well and good – but de Valera would find that, as negotia-tions began with imperial Britain, it was rather easier to don a Republican Presidential cloak in Philadelphia than it was in Downing Street.

It is also the case that the genuine adulation which he was accorded in America was significantly overvalued in Ireland – for de Valera actually achieved very little of substance behind the smokescreen of publicity; in addition to which, his methods caused both disruption to the Irish cause, and antagonism from those who should by right have been his firm allies. His empha-sis, for example, on insisting that Irish policies be determined by him alone, without interference from other Irish-American leaders, led to serious tension and splits – as a result of which neither the Democratic nor the Republican parties included an Irish plank in their Presidential programmes for 1920. In addi-tion, while de Valera was given great credit in Ireland for having raised some five million dollars in a bond to fund the struggle for Irish freedom, what was not widely understood was that he had left some sixty percent of this money lying in American banks – and that most of this would in the future be channelled towards the establishment of the de Valera-controlled *Irish Press* newspaper. To be sure, most of his supporters regarded this as being part of The Cause, part of a continuing effort to fill the vision of 1916. But in fact, he kept the paper under his personal control – making of it a family asset.

But this was for the future. In the early days of 1921, and within two weeks of being installed in a safe house by Collins, de Valera demonstrated the power of his ego, and the strength of his vision of his own importance to the conduct of the struggle. He made an attempt to get Collins out of Ireland to America, ostensibly to take his place in generating publicity. But an appalled Collins, realising that the intelligence war would collapse without him, declared bluntly that 'the long hoor won't get rid of me that easily' – and turned down this particular poisoned chalice.

The other major de Valera policy initiative involved an attempt to have the war fought on different lines. He told Collins and Mulcahy that the assassinations and the ambushes were having a bad effect in America; instead, he said, he favoured the idea of one good battle every month, with about five hundred on either side. History does not record how it was intended to get the British not to exceed their quota of five hundred men – but even if such engagements had been possible, the effect would have been to wipe out the IRA within a few months. The organisation's lightly armed flying columns and active service units depended on secrecy, and on succour in the hills and homes of Ireland: and once they emerged from such fastnesses, the Volunteers would have been swept away rapidly by a well-equipped and battle-hardened regular army.

It was, then, an astonishingly bad strategic idea – and yet de Valera would not let it go, continuing to push for large-scale manoeuvres that would have destroyed the Apostles. Such an effect may not, it is true, have been part of his calculations – but it is certainly the case that he sought continuously to get control of the army: even to the extent of trying to set up a new army which would take a new oath to the Dáil and *ipso facto* the President of the Dáil – that is to say, de Valera himself.

Parallel to this attempt at developing a new military policy, meanwhile, de Valera also began emphasising the importance of the underground Dáil, by increasing the number of its meetings under himself as President. And at the same time, he began cultivating a strategic friendship with Collins's two principal enemies within the cabinet, Cathal Brugha and Austin Stack. Collins of course could not but be aware of these developments – and it seems to me that they must have been a wearisome burden to a man already pursuing an exhausting underground war from the saddle of a bicycle which took him to a different hiding place, through road blocks and searches, to a brief sleep in a different house every night.

But there were other developments that must have been rather more cheering for Collins. Underground movements towards an honourable peace were gathering momentum now – and the efforts of the businessman Patrick Moylett, the senior civil servant Alfred Cope and the murdered Conor

Clune's uncle, the Catholic Archbishop of Perth, Joseph Clune, now visiting Ireland, would begin to pay dividends. One such was the realisation by Lloyd George, as a result of conversations with intermediaries, that Collins was not merely an enemy with which to be reckoned – but a man of considerable calibre, and a possible partner in peace. Clune also made the Prime Minister more aware than he had previously been the case of the predations of the Auxiliaries and the Black and Tans, and the frightful impact they were having on Irish public opinion.

The work of Cope in particular deserves praise and reassessment. He was a man of courage and merit – and his activities in the direction of peace brought upon him the suspicions of his own side. As for Collins: he saw Cope as a pleasant English gentleman but he was inevitably wary of the peace feelers. His fundamental attitude was that, as T. Ryle Dwyer quotes in his *Michael Collins and the Civil War* (2012):

There will be no compromise and we will have no negotiations with any British government until Ireland is recognised as an independent Republic. I see you think we have only to whittle our demand down to Dominion Home Rule and we shall get it. The talk about Dominion Home Rule is not promoted by England with a view to granting it to us, but merely with a view to getting rid of the Republican movement. England will give us neither as a gift. The same effort that has sold us Dominion Home Rule will get us a Republic.

They were tough words – but de Valera's presence in Ireland, his demands and his autocratic ways meant that the ground was now shifting beneath Collins's feet. In particular, de Valera had his way in one disastrous matter: for it was decided that a dramatic set-piece attack on a landmark building was the very thing that the Republican cause needed. The destruction of an iconic Dublin landmark, said de Valera, would both attest to the strength of the IRA and capture world headlines.

The landmark chosen was the Custom House, James Gandon's fine building beside the Liffey – and the date chosen was 25 May 1921. De Valera seems to have thought this would be a relatively easy target, because the British had withdrawn their guard on the building a little earlier. Relatively easy – but still fraught with peril, for there were troops and military vehicles all over the city. The ill-judged attack on the Custom House was the nearest thing to one of de Valera's set-piece proposals to occur during the entire war of independence. It was also the most costly for the IRA.

Collins had a bad feeling about the operation and tried, in fact, to prevent Squad involvement. Tom Ennis of the Dublin Battalion, however, managed to have Collins's objections overruled. The long-standing Squad leader Paddy Daly also tried to have the Squad arrangements altered – but in his case, he wanted *more* rather than less participation. He felt that all members of the Squad should be included – and he got his way, although Collins did manage to secure the exclusion of many of the people from Crow Street and other senior intelligence figures. Dan McDonnell recalled Collins giving strict instructions that 'on no account' were McDonnell and his senior colleagues to go near the Custom House that day. McDonnell said afterwards that Collins's public reasoning was that he didn't want everybody involved in the operation. By 'involved', Collins clearly meant captured.

The Squad – twenty members in all – was placed in charge of the entrances to the Custom House. Their instructions were to let out nobody who had been visiting or working in the building, and to keep out anyone who turned up when the raid was in progress. A group who were explicitly not expected to turn up were the Black and Tans – as a heavy force of the Dublin Brigade were deployed in the environs of the Custom House to prevent either the Tans or unwanted fire brigades aborting the action. The Custom House operation, however, was subjected to a heavy dose of bad luck almost from the outset. In the first place – as might have been expected, given the large numbers of troops roaming the streets – a large party of Tans *did* turn up unexpectedly, and they surrounded the building. Secondly, the lorry containing the paraffin intended to ignite the building was delayed – meaning that petrol, which is more dangerous to use, had to be deployed instead. In addition, other cracks in the plan soon developed. Ennis, for example, found that he had not enough men to carry out the burning duties: it should have been obvious beforehand that it would take a great deal of manpower to speedily enter and burn every room in the huge Custom House and still manage to get away safely – but apparently it was not, underscoring yet again what a botched job this was always going to be. Before long, questions were being asked: what was going on? Where were the flames? Then, a lorry containing Black and Tans pulled up beside the building. One of the Volunteers lobbed a hand grenade into the lorry – and it exploded, throwing Tans out of the lorry. Firing broke out – but now it became clear that the rebels' plan was failing: the Tans were able to take up their station without coming under fire. British security units were also able to roust out firemen from nearby Tara Street fire station, whom the IRA had earlier warned not to attend the blaze.

Inside the building, things were going no better. Vinnie Byrne was assigned to the destruction of some of the second-floor offices – but upstairs he ran into difficulties which should also have been anticipated. One office was occupied by a pair of clerks, a man and a woman. Byrne 'requested them to leave', giving in response to their quite reasonable queries as to why they should do this the equally valid answer that he intended to set the place on fire. Byrne recalls laconically that 'the guy got very worried about the whole thing' – the fact that Byrne produced a revolver to underline the seriousness of his remarks may have accounted for the man's anxiety. The woman, meanwhile, focused on her priorities, asking whether she could take her coat? – to which Byrne replied that she would be lucky to get out with her life, a remark which considerably expedited the lady's departure.

The building did eventually go up in flames – but the security forces had managed to ring the entire precinct, and clusters of Squad members were arrested. When the dust settled on the operation, in fact, it was discovered that over eighty Volunteers had been captured – and included were most of the Squad. One, Sean Doyle, died of his wounds. Paddy Daly and Oscar Traynor got the badly wounded leader of the raid, Tom Ennis, safely to a friendly nursing home in Eccles Street despite being stopped by a police cordon.

Six members of the Dublin IRA's active service unit were killed. While pictures of the burning Custom House flashed around the world for several days after the attack, the value of this publicity has to be weighed against the human cost. Certainly, had the IRA embarked on such tactics earlier in the struggle, the story of the Twelve Apostles would have been a short one. Lodged among the plethora of dry figures and statistics, however, are some remarkable human stories. Amongst those captured, for example, were two prominent Kilkenny Volunteers Tommy Kilcoyne and Paddy Swanzy – who gave false names to their captors, pretending to be brothers, Tommy and Paddy Lewis. Had they been identified, both men knew that their lives were at risk. Daly and Traynor came up with a plan to secure their release: they arranged to make it appear that the mother of the captured men was dying, in the expectation that her sons would be released for a last visit – and a friendly doctor provided a certificate that the phantom Mrs Lewis was indeed dying of a heart condition at 17 North Richmond Street.

When a policeman arrived at the house to check on the health of this 'Mrs Lewis', they disturbed the actual occupant, a Mrs Byrne, who was in the middle of baking. She was, recalls Daly, a 'very stout woman, who had twelve children': and now she ran up four flights of stairs without stopping to wash the flour from her hands, and jumped into bed in order to play the part of the dying Mrs Lewis. The curtains in the room were half-drawn, allegedly to spare the dying woman's eyes – and naturally she kept her floury hands under the bedclothes. The rush upstairs, however, had winded the unfortunate woman – and as the policeman entered the room, she was genuinely gasping and seemed very ill indeed. The policeman was sympathetic and went off to report that 'Mrs Lewis' was indeed *in articulo mortis*. Meanwhile, fearing that a military doctor might be sent to check on the patient in the wake of the police visit, Daly arranged for Mrs Byrne to be transferred to the Mater Private hospital under the guise of the dying 'Mrs Lewis'.

Now, however, a new problem arose. One of Tommy Kilcoyne's sisters, knowing that he was using the name Lewis, sent him a telegram saying that his mother was dead. 'Now,' writes Daly with unconscious humour, 'we were in a fix: we could get a dying woman easily enough, but where would we get a corpse?' Indeed, this must have been one of the few occasions on which the Squad found it impossible to provide a corpse. In the event, and while the problem was being debated, the sympathetic policeman came back and knocked on the door to inform the occupants that the 'Lewis' boys were being released on compassionate grounds, and could be expected home shortly. They went home – but to Kilkenny, where they remained safely.

In the shocked aftermath of the Custom House raid, meanwhile, Collins stood drinks for a few of the survivors in Kirwan's public house on Parnell Street – and Dan McDonnell, one of those who partook of his hospitality, remarked with considerable understatement that the boss was 'not too happy about the results'. Collins had good reason to be unhappy: de Valera's Custom House catastrophe could be said to have marked the end of the Twelve Apostles as an elite unit. The remaining members of the unit were amalgamated under Paddy Daly into the active service unit of the Dublin Brigade, which became known as the Dublin Guard. The new formation was not universally popular: two former leading members of the active service unit, Paddy Flanagan and Mick White, resigned; and while Crow Street was still intact, the Guards were encouraged to find their own targets, subject to Daly's approval. The Apostles' old aura and prestige was greatly diminished.

Diminished – though not wholly destroyed: indeed, the Dublin IRA retained a great deal of lethal potential. A month or so later, for example, an operation was planned which – had it come off – would have put Bloody Sunday quite in the shade. It was arranged that every Auxiliary or Tan on the streets of Dublin was to be targeted; in addition to which, a Squad under Frank Thornton was to go into Kidd's Back and shoot every Tan, informer or Auxiliary in sight. At the last moment, however, the operation was called off. Some, including Paddy Daly, claim that the reason was that de Valera felt the operation might have damaged the peace negotiations which would prove to bear fruit in a truce that lay only two weeks away in the future. Thornton, however, claims that the plan was called off because unexpected army patrols had blocked routes of escape and that ammunition was in short supply. Yet the very fact that such a scheme was in the works in the first place is evidence that the IRA was far from defeated.

In the meantime, the world had changed again. There was now a new political reality in Ireland, albeit one that was not treated with the importance it should have been by the Sinn Féin movement. This new political reality would embody something that had almost been lost sight of by the hard-pressed Sinn Féiners. Ireland was now effectively partitioned. Indeed, a mere month after the attack on the Custom House, King George V arrived in Belfast to inaugurate the new Unionist-dominated parliament representing six Ulster counties. Effectively speaking, the Unionists had achieved what they had envisaged all along in their plans to declare a provisional government in Ulster should Home Rule come to pass. They had not succeeded in their primary aim of frustrating the introduction of Home Rule entirely, of course – but still, half a loaf was better than no bread at all. Within this new entity of Northern Ireland Unionists now had an area within which Catholics and Nationalists could be coerced by means of discrimination in employment and gerrymandering in elections. So far as the Tory and Unionist strategists were concerned, then, they had won: even though Ulster had not actually fought, Ulster had been right.

The speech delivered by the king on 7 June 1921 had originally been written by Balfour: and it has been described as a 'bloodthirsty' document. It had to be toned down – and Lloyd George was persuaded that a more emollient and less offensive speech might help to bring the war in Ireland to an end. Accordingly, the king read out a generally conciliatory speech written for him by the South African leader Jan Smuts who was in London for a conference.

> It is my earnest desire that in Southern Ireland there may, ere long, take place a parallel to what is now passing in this hall, that there a similar occasion may present itself, and a similar ceremony be performed. For this the Parliament of the United Kingdom has in the fullest measure provided the powers; for this the Parliament of Ulster is pointing the way.

Collins warned that once hostilities ceased, the IRA would be like 'rabbits coming out of their holes'. Their greatest weapon was secrecy – and it would at a stroke be gone. But he soon had other things to concern him – as de Valera now delivered the greatest blow he had inflicted on Collins since his return from America. He took with him a delegation to London to begin negotiations with the British government: the delegation included Austin Stack – but Collins himself was excluded. Collins protested vehemently against this stroke – but he was overridden by de Valera, who said that if Collins accompanied the delegation it would provide the British with opportunities of photographing him. The fact that one of de Valera's first gestures on arriving back from America had been to try to get

Collins to go there, thus providing extensive opportunities for photography, appeared to have been conveniently forgotten.

De Valera subsequently left the members of his delegation to sightsee in London, while he spent days alone with Lloyd George in Downing Street, learning what the British planned for the remaining twenty-six counties of Southern Ireland. The new state, Lloyd George told de Valera, was to have the same constitutional status as Australia, New Zealand, Newfoundland and Canada. It would have its own parliament, army, civil service and control over internal affairs, excise duties and all other forms of taxation. But, and this turned out to be a very big but, members of the new parliament would have to take an oath of allegiance to the king. A Governor General would represent the king in this new Irish Free State. Partition would remain. This new Dominion was not the thirty-two county Republic envisaged in the Proclamation of 1916 but (as Collins himself would later claim with justice) the deal could be used as a 'stepping stone' to full independence. For the fiery young men of the IRA, however, it was bound to be a difficult proposition to accept – and certainly de Valera shrank from the prospect of trying to gain their acceptance. Instead, he decided that Collins should lead the next delegation to London to plot the tortuous path towards a peace treaty. As J. B. E. Hittle writes, de Valera's failure to participate in the Treaty talks ranks among 'the most cowardly political acts in history'.

This period, then, from July to October 1921, would prove to be of the great importance both to the future of Ireland, and to the future Anglo-Irish relationship. It was a fraught phase of dangerous, nerve-stretching shadow boxing, with the British attempting to hold the Irish to the agreement spelled out verbally and in writing to de Valera during his conclaves with Lloyd George in London. The Irish, meanwhile, sought to evade the reality that a Republic was not to be had through procrastination and the exchange of correspondence which mopped up time, but brought neither negotiation nor settlement any nearer. In addition, while this agonising process was taking place, nobody talked about the presence of the elephant in the room: for the partition of Ireland was now a fact, not merely in a *de facto* sense, but *de jure*.

In September, a final exchange of position papers took place: and it contained now the basis for an Irish delegation to come to London to conclude a formal peace agreement. The British position contained a declaration that:

> His Majesty's Government [...] cannot enter negotiation on the basis of this correspondence [...] on this point they must guard themselves against any possible doubt. We, therefore, send you a *fresh* [author's italics] invitation to a conference in London on 11 October, where we can meet your delegation as spokesmen for the people whom you represent with a view to ascertaining how the association of Ireland with the community of nations known as the British Empire may be reconciled with Irish national aspirations.

And from the Irish side:

We have received your invitation to a Conference in London on October 11th with a view to ascertaining how the association of Ireland with the community of nations known as the British Empire may best be reconciled with Irish national aspirations. Our respective positions have been stated and are understood, and we agree that conference, not correspondence, is the most practical and hopeful way to understanding. We accept the invitation [...] and our delegates will meet you in London to explore every possibility of settlement by personal discussion.

Quite clearly – and quite frankly – there was not a snowball's chance in hell of the Irish producing a thirty-two-county Republic within such a framework. No one realised this better, of course, than the one man in Europe who had sat alone for day-long conferences with Lloyd George while the proposed deal was spelled out to him. But de Valera found a way out of facing the truth of the situation; he resolved that he would not go back to London again to face the music – and he decided that instead he would send Michael Collins and Arthur Griffith.

Collins knew immediately he was being presented with one of the larger poisoned chalices in the history of Anglo-Irish relations: but having argued strenuously against going, he finally allowed himself to be persuaded. Collins was a supreme realist, and he knew that if the truce was not capitalised on at this point, valuable momentum would be lost. Equally, he understood that if hostilities were resumed, the British would now have the equally inestimable advantage of being able to identify both himself and his underground army with relative ease. (This was because the much enlarged British intelligence operations had had a relatively free hand during the truce.) To London, then, Collins was bound in that autumn of 1921. His title of 'plenipotentiary' ceded him the authority to negotiate largely as he saw fit: and this aspect too had been approved by de Valera, the better to limit his own exposure to what was likely to be a messy business.

While these negotiations were in progress between October and December, de Valera and Brugha went about the country conducting a military-tinged charade: that of inspecting the Volunteers on parade as though they formed a regular stand-ing army. The reality was, of course, that the bravery of these young recruits would not have sustained them for a week in open warfare with a heavily armed and numerically superior British army. This fact can readily enough be ascertained from later events: from, in particular, the speed with which the Republican side would be overwhelmed by the better armed Free State army in the Civil War. Such would have been the indubitable fate of de Valera's unfortunate recruits too, had the truce ended not in the peace that Collins had been despatched to London purportedly to bring about, but in the Anglo-Irish war that would rapidly have followed had he failed.

In essence, de Valera was attempting to use Collins's absence to undermine his rival's position. So much is clear from his activ-ities at this time: he was not only drilling 'his' army, but trying to reorganise it in such a way as to diminish Collins's influence, and enhance his own. With this in mind, de Valera sought to force what he called the 'New Army' to swear allegiance specifically to the Dáil (of which he was of course President), rather than to the IRB, which was governed by Collins. But when he met with the officer corps of GHQ to inform them of what was essentially a *diktat,* he discovered the limitations of his influence. His timing, for one thing, could not have been better – or worse: this was 25 November 1921, and Collins and Griffith were now on a boat back to Britain to conclude the final Treaty negotiations, on which (let us not forget) de Valera had given them no clear guidance – and Collins's men felt the insult for their boss. Now, therefore, speaking for the rest of the officers, J. J. 'Ginger' O'Connell told de Valera that there was no need for re-organisation. The men in the room had all risked their lives together and were like 'a band of brothers'.

De Valera realised that though Collins was not present in the room, his influence most certainly was. His initial response was to throw the disturbing sort of nervous fit he had previously displayed during his American tour, when he was trying to overthrow the established Irish-American leadership. He flew into an ungovernable rage: jumping up, he pushed away the table in front of him, and 'half screaming half shouting', blurted out the statement: 'Ye may mutiny if ye like, but Ireland will give me another Army!' However, even de Valera realised that he had gone too far. With peace hanging in the balance (it was clear to all that matters were coming to a head in London), this was no time to antagonise GHQ – and de Valera eventually abandoned his New Army proposals. This incident, however, will forever stand as an example of how, even at a time of national emergency, he was prepared to subordinate national goals to his own instinct for power. It also underscores the solidarity and loyalty that Collins was able to inspire in his colleagues: after all, when the anti-Treatyites attempted to fight the Free State Army in the months ahead, they were facing virtually that same 'band of brothers', the fraternal cohesion of which practically guaranteed success.

The final Treaty settlement would prove to be based squarely on the London proposals of July. The main points were that the twenty-six counties of Southern Ireland would form a self-governing Dominion within the Empire – but with the six counties of Northern Ireland excluded from this new state; the monarch would remain Irish head of state, and as such all Irish legislators would be required to swear an oath of allegiance to the crown; and the so-called Irish 'Treaty Ports' – strategically significant deep-water harbours in Counties Donegal and Cork – would be retained for use by the Royal Navy. As late as three days before the document was signed, Griffith and Collins had returned to Dublin to brief a long and inconclusive meeting of the Dáil at which these facts and details were foreshadowed.

Although there was acrimony in plenty, agreement or even guidance as to what might be sought remained conspicuous by its absence – and Griffith and Collins returned to London no wiser than when they had left it. De Valera had, after all, deliberately built dissension into the London delegation: and this manifested itself in the manner in which the delegation travelled back to the negotiations. Griffith and Collins travelled on one boat to Holyhead, while their fellow plenipotentiaries Robert Barton, Gavan Duffy, Eamonn Duggan and Erskine Childers sailed in another. These travel arrangements merely underscored what had by then become an accepted state of affairs: throughout the negotiations, Collins and Griffith had conducted play by subcommittee so as to exclude in particular Childers, whom they regarded both as needlessly obstructive and as acting as de Valera's mouthpiece and spy.

Throughout the months of negotiation, of course, de Valera had deliberately avoided discussing the content of the emerging agreement. Collins, who effectively led the delegation in London because of Griffith's poor health, had made repeated return trips to Dublin in the course of the negotiations to keep in contact with the IRB and his fiancée Kitty Kiernan, not necessarily in that order. He could have been contacted at any point. Subsequent to the signing of the Treaty, however, de Valera continued to maintain that he had had no knowledge of its contents until he read them in an evening paper in Dublin after the Treaty itself had been signed in the early hours of 6 December 1921. He further maintained that the signing without his authorisation was an act of treachery unparalleled in history.

This in fact is not true. While the Treaty was being signed de Valera was staying at the home of Stephen O'Meara in Limerick with – amongst others – the former IRA chief of staff and now General Richard Mulcahy. A phone call came to the house from London for Mulcahy, informing him of the Treaty's details. Mulcahy listened and then turning to de Valera, asked him would he like to talk to the caller. He refused, saying,

'I didn't think that they [the British] would give in so easily.' Significantly, as newspaper boys were selling newspapers on the streets of Limerick containing the terms of the historic settlement, de Valera preserved his pose of ignorance and travelled back to Dublin not with Mulcahy and his ADC, but with Cathal Brugha. When the Treaty signatory Eamonn Duggan arrived on the evening of 6 December at the Mansion House, where a ceremony commemorating Dante was being held, de Valera refused to accept the copy of the Treaty which Duggan had rushed to give him, saying: 'What, signed, whether I was consulted or not!' Newspapers had been on sale in Dublin for hours before de Valera attended the Dante ceremony – and yet throughout his life de Valera maintained the fiction that he had no knowledge of the Treaty's contents until he was shown them in an evening newspaper an hour before the Dante ceremony began.

A concentration on the creator of *Inferno* proved an appropriate prelude for what was to befall. De Valera's initial reaction was to try and have Collins and Griffith arrested. He thought he had a majority of cabinet members with him, for he expected that W. T. Cosgrave would join with Brugha and Stack in supporting him – but Cosgrave demurred, saying that the point of view of the negotiators should be heard first. The signing of the Treaty, meanwhile, had been greeted with relief amongst the public at large. In the evenings before it was concluded, the British had saturated the streets with troops once more – and the threat of renewed warfare had inevitably created a national anxiety which the news of the signing now alleviated. Consequently there was considerable shock and con-fusion when de Valera issued a statement declaring that:

> The terms of this agreement are in violent conflict with the wishes of the majority of this nation, as expressed freely in successive elections during the past three years. I feel it my duty to inform you immediately that I cannot recommend the acceptance of this Treaty either to Dáil Éireann or to the country. I am supported by the Ministers of Home Affairs and Defence...

But when Erskine Childers asked him where he could expect to find support for his stand against the Treaty, de Valera made a fateful response which was to govern his behaviour until he founded his own party Fianna Fáil (the 'Warriors of Destiny', established in 1926) – and indeed for years after-wards. He told Childers, as the latter noted in his diary on 9 December 1921, that he would look for strength from 'extrem-ist support'. Certainly it was the case that a large segment of the IRA – indeed, probably the majority – rejected the terms of the Treaty: yet it was never explained to them or the public at large, either in the Dáil or anywhere else, how the partition of the country might be dealt with. Instead, de Valera (and everyone else) dealt with the issue of Partition by ignoring it, focusing instead on Ruritanian questions to do with the oath of allegiance; the status of the Governor General (the king's new representative) in Ireland; and general issues to do with the trappings of imperialism. These were topics little calculated to exercise the Irish public – yet it was, remarkably, on such issues that de Valera's rejection of the Treaty ostensibly turned. The acrimonious Dáil debate continued until 7 January 1922, when the Treaty was carried by 64 to 57. The narrowness of the majority in the Dáil was not reflected amongst the public at large – but Collins's previous initiative with Harry Boland in rigging the Sinn Féin candidates' lists with radical 'forward' individuals (see page 60) had now come home to roost. The temper of many of those inside the Dáil was considerably more militant than in the world outside.

De Valera reacted to the vote by leading his supporters out of the Dáil, thereby leaving the new state without a government. But though he continued to characterise the Dáil as a 'usurping constitution', and re-entered it whenever he wanted to make a statement or oppose a vote, it became clear that the public at large supported the Treaty. The half-loaf of the new Irish Free State was, it seemed, preferable to the no-bread of the Republic – and in the elections held on 16 June 1922, pro-Treaty parties would secure over 75% of the vote. Many prominent IRA leaders, however, did not support the Treaty: and throughout the spring and early summer of 1922 they began seizing strongpoints and funding their operations by raids on banks and post offices.

Throughout this period too, de Valera continued his quest for 'extremist support'. In March, he delivered a series of as what became known as 'wading through blood' speeches. At an event at Dungarvan on 16 March, he claimed that 'the Treaty […] barred the way to Independence with the blood of fellow Irishmen [...] it was only by civil war after this that they could get their Independence. [...] if you don't fight today you will have to fight tomorrow [...] and I say, when you are in a good fighting position, then fight on.' The next day, in Carrick-on-Suir, he repeated this argument, and at Thurles later that same day he said:

> Those who want complete freedom from such as we armed for before must not meet only foreign soldiers, but the forces of their own countrymen who support the Free State Government. If the Treaty is ratified, you who are propos-ing to achieve freedom must march over the dead bodies of your own brothers. You must wade through Irish blood.

In view of what was to befall later – in the course of the Civil War, and especially in County Kerry – what de Valera had to say in Killarney on 18 March is of particular importance:

> In order to achieve freedom if our Volunteers continue, *and I hope they will continue until the goal is reached* [...] then these men in order to achieve freedom will have, I said yesterday, to march over the dead bodies of their own brothers. They will have to wade through Irish blood.

He abandoned this line of argument after the *Irish Independent* published some of his utterances, leading to widespread criticism of his use of inflammatory language. It was toned down accord-ingly – although relatively undaunted, de Valera attempted to bluster that the policy of the *Independent* was 'villainous'. His extremist words and policies did, however, achieve some of his ends – in particular he was able to form relationships with leaders of the rejectionist faction of the IRA. One of these was Rory O'Connor, who in April 1922 made good on his own rejectionist tendencies by leading the occupation of the landmark Four Courts building in central Dublin – an action that would in time lead to devastating consequences.

Collins, meanwhile, was equivocating as to the best courses of action. Members of the rejectionist faction had until lately been his own brothers in arms: and now they were occupying buildings and raiding post offices and banks as a means of financing their campaign against the lawful government of the Free State. Now, and to add to his difficulties, the enraged British delivered an ultimatum: either to eject O'Connor and his company from the Four Courts (which had been provocatively chosen, because it was the nerve-centre of the Irish legal system), or the British would do it for him. And so Collins began to lay his plans for an assault on his former comrades.

A number of other events, meanwhile, had conspired to make outright civil war inevitable. Collins had concluded a desperate and essentially anti-democratic pact with de Valera which would have allowed the latter, together with Childers, Brugha, Stack and others to contest the elections called for by the Treaty under the shared banner of Sinn Féin. By the terms of this accord, voters would have been asked to select from a panel composed of two sets of Sinn Féin opinion, both pro- and anti-Treaty. Griffith – like many others – was dismayed by such an arrangement. Apart from the fact that it could have placed in government anti-Treaty figures like Childers and de Valera, it cut across the interests of other political groupings in the country; and furthermore it had been set in place without being agreed by the cabinet. Collins's aim was to buy time for the completion of a new constitution, which he hoped could be made Republican enough to satisfy both wings of the IRA. This new document was singular in that it did not envisage an oath of allegiance either to the monarch or to a Governor General.

The British, however, rejected the constitution out of hand, with Churchill describing it as being 'Bolshevik in character'. The constitution was revised to the satisfaction of the imperialists and the dissatisfaction of the Republicans – and, having failed in his attempt to make the constitution acceptable to the Republicans, Collins repudiated the pact on the eve of the election. He asked the people simply to vote for the candidates they preferred best; and the result following the election of 16 June, showed an overwhelming majority for the Treaty. Peace now hung by a frayed thread.

CHAPTER TEN

Drift to Disaster

A Dublin crowd watches the battle of the Four Courts on the corner of Capel Street Bridge and Parliament Street, June 1922.

M ICHAEL COLLINS WAS NOW EMBROILED IN A TENSE AND rapidly escalating political situation south of the new Irish border. This did not, however, mean that he had lost sight of the dream of an all-island Republic that had motivated his Squad for month after month and year after year – and he demonstrated this in a decision he made that same dangerous summer of 1922. On 22 June, Sir Henry Wilson was assassinated on the doorstep of his central London home by two IRA Volunteers, Reggie Dunne and Joseph O'Sullivan – and it is virtually certain that Collins ordered the assassination. Wilson, we may recall, was one of the most important figures in the British armed forces, and a figure, therefore, at the heart of the British establishment: he had played a central role in the conduct of the Great War; he had been a military representative at the post-war talks at Versailles – and he had been intimately involved in all British military and political responses to the War of Independence in Ireland.

Now, as a fiercely anti-Catholic pogrom was raging in Belfast, Wilson was principal advisor to Northern Ireland Prime Minister Sir James Craig – and was widely held to be responsible for the anti-Catholic policies that held sway in the infant Northern Ireland. Collins may have had his hands full at this time – but he was determined just the same to make an example of one or more of the Unionist elite north of the border – and Wilson, as a consistent anti-Nationalist voice since the time of the Curragh mutiny era almost a decade previously, and in the words of Collins himself a 'violent Orange partisan', was the chosen target. The killers were apprehended and hanged: and the Wilson assassination had the effect of causing a wave of horror and anger to pass through the British establishment. Because it was speculated – wrongly – that anti-Treaty personnel had been behind the killing, the British government resolved now to press Collins and the Irish authorities to deal once and for all with the festering situation at the Four Courts.

A week later, on 28 June 1922, using an 18-pound military piece borrowed from the British, Collins fired on the Four Courts. He acted thus with a heavy heart, because his regard for O'Connor and many of the other anti-Treaty Commanders was far higher than that for many of his cabinet colleagues and he had gone to great lengths in an attempt to avoid hostilities. Circumstances, however, had now forced his hand. Open warfare now returned to the streets of central Dublin: the Four Courts, and much of its environs, was destroyed; and in the process a millennium of records kept by the Irish Public Record Office (housed at the rear of the building) went up in smoke. De Valera, meanwhile, greeted the assault on the building by issuing a Proclamation:

Young men and young women of Ireland: hold steadily on. Those who with cries of woe and lamentation would now involve you in a disastrous rout, you will soon see rally behind you and vie with you for first place in the vanguard. Beyond all telling is the destiny God has in mind for Ireland, the fair, the peerless one. You are the artificers of that destiny. Yours is the faith that moves mountains, the faith that confounds misgivings. Yours is the faith and love that begot the enterprise of 1916. Young men and young women of Ireland, the goal is at last in sight – steady, altogether forward. Ireland is yours for the taking. Take it.

De Valera then re-joined the IRA, claiming to be an ordinary Volunteer. However, this was surely a disingenuous claim: Dan Breen – who could be relied upon when it came to all matters Tipperary – recalls that after the Anti-Treaty IRA had vacated the town of Cashel following a temporary occupation, de Valera possessed sufficient authority with the Volunteers to send them back in again to retake the town. Indeed, far from being a mere Volunteer who had simply re-joined the ranks when firing commenced on the Four Courts, de Valera was in fact Director of Operations when he handed over this senior post to Tom Barry. But by the time he did so, the IRA was clearly being defeated. In addition, it is worth noting that some of the operations which have been ascribed to de Valera were acts of rank destruction; these include the severing of the crucial Dublin–Cork rail link at Mallow.

The destruction of the Four Courts is perhaps the most infamous act of Ireland's fratricidal civil war – but it was only one of many vicious episodes. All such civil strife is of course by its nature savage – and the war in Ireland was no exception. By the time Michael Collins was killed in an ambush at Béal na Bláth in County Cork in August 1922, it had already become evident to all that the pro-Treaty side was bound to win the gathering conflict – yet it dragged on regardless, and with hate-filled destructiveness, until the following May. Richard Mulcahy succeeded Collins as Commander in Chief of the Army – and inexorably he crushed the resistance of a Republican side which, though it lacked nothing in courage and idealism, wanted both the military skill and the popular support necessary to win a war. Those men holed up in the Four Courts – to give just one example – had assumed that they could slip out of the burning complex using an underground tunnel which issued on the banks of the river Liffey. They realised too late that this reach of the Liffey in central Dublin is tidal – and that their escape route was blocked by ten or twelve feet of water. In Dublin also, another fundamental blunder occurred when Republican troops attempting to reach the Anti-Treaty headquarters in the Hammam building on Sackville Street rendered their task mission impossible – by conducting their tunnelling operations on the wrong side of the street.

The factor, however, that truly stands out in terms of Pro-Treaty effectiveness was the sheer ruthless efficiency of the methods employed – and these were methods which, as we shall see shortly, some of the former Apostles played a distinctly inglorious part in executing. The Pro-Treaty leadership certainly did not consist of shrinking violets: Mulcahy was joined by Cosgrave, with Kevin O'Higgins as a particularly ferocious enforcer. They could count on the backing of the Catholic Church too: the Hierarchy issued a pastoral letter condemning the Republicans in forthright terms, and threatening to excommunicate them; and they in turn were backed by the powerful farming and business lobbies.

In the violent summer and autumn of 1922, the energies of the Squad were poured into what might be termed the 'reprisal factor' of the Civil War. Collins himself, just a few weeks before his death on 22 August, is on record as favouring the shooting of looters and reprisals against Republican attacks – in this case a bold assault on a prison train at Killurin in County Wexford on 24 July, which resulted in the deaths of two Free State soldiers. One of Collins's last public appearances, indeed, was to attend the funeral of eight members of the Pro-Treaty forces blown up by a Republican mine. One of the victims of this attack was his old friend and prominent Squad member Tom Keogh – whose death left a very bitter taste in the mouths of his colleagues.

This literally murderous anger found its expression in many forms of violent reprisal in locales across the country – and in Dublin and County Kerry in particular. In Dublin, practically the entire Squad was enrolled in what became known as Oriel House, which in effect functioned as the new Crow Street intelligence operation and the new Irish Criminal Investigation Department (CID) combined; and which was based in the eponymous building on Dublin's Westland Row. A series of familiar names gathered at Oriel House, including Liam Tobin, who was both a general in the new Free State Army and controller of Oriel House intelligence-gathering; other survivors including Tom Cullen, Charlie Dalton and Frank Saurin; and such former spies in the Castle as Ned Broy, Jim McNamara and David Neligan – all of whom had chosen to follow Collins himself in accepting an imperfect Treaty.

The various intelligence-gathering and CID activities associated with Oriel House were entrusted to the leadership of Joseph McGrath, a tough survivor of 1916, who in the future would become one of Ireland's most successful businessmen. The Oriel House organisation soon established a reputation for brutal efficiency: it is reckoned to have committed at least twenty-five extra-judicial killings in the course of Ireland's period of internecine strife. In retaliation, a lesser number of Oriel House detectives, possibly three in all, were shot. The Oriel House operation was wound up in November 1923 – this, after the Civil War had ended and the unit's activities had passed a point where any government could defend them. Oriel House's activities, indeed, can only be understood, although not forgiven, by the circumstances of the time. These had persuaded the Free State government to introduce emergency legislation to cope with the deteriorating security situation – and in particular, as we will see, to ensure the execution of one man, Erskine Childers.

It is true that the security and stability of the infant Free State were fragile in the extreme. It was beset by enemies south and north of the border; and, in addition, there were many in high places in Britain who would have welcomed any opportunity to undermine its economic and security credibility. It would certainly appear that the Free State cabinet accepted the harsh policy suggestions of Kevin O'Higgins who in July 1922 noted that, 'what was needed to put down the Irregulars [Republicans] were more local executions and we should just kill them anyway'. It must be noted here that part of O'Higgins's motivation was not mere ruthlessness, but the fact that in addition to Anti-Treaty sentiment, some of these 'Irregulars' were supporting land agitation. With cattle prices low and rents going unpaid, cattle-rustling and land seizure were becoming part of the ongoing unrest. Fears were expressed at cabinet, particularly by Minister for Agriculture Patrick Hogan, that a new and potentially anarchic land war was on the verge of erupting – and it was to cope with such a threat that a special corps was formed within Oriel House. The Special Infantry Corps was a ruthlessly efficient body, and it succeeded in curbing this unrest on the land. The new – and unarmed – Garda Síochána was as a result able to move into areas of the country which had not seen a policeman since 1919, when attacks first began on the RIC.

It is emphatically the case that this period of Irish history does not make for comfortable study. In fact, it is very difficult to make any study of it at all, because so many records of the period were deliberately destroyed before power was eventually handed over peacefully to de Valera in 1932. After all, handing power over was one thing, handing over a body of evidence which could have incriminated his political enemies quite another. And it is certainly part of the folklore of the period that the skies above police headquarters in the Phoenix

Park were illuminated for several nights by the flames of documents burned by order of the outgoing Free State Minister for Defence, Desmond Fitzgerald.

While documentary evidence is hard to come by, however, I have in the course of my research heard many stories of torture by members of the Oriel House team. These cannot, by their nature, be wholly verified – but it seems to me that many have the ring of truth. One eyewitness account was given to me by the veteran Republican Joseph Clarke, who described how he saw a suspect in Oriel House itself, his entrails protruding from his anus after a kicking. Another story concerns Alf Colley and Séan Cole, two youthful members of Fianna Éireann (in effect, Republican boy scouts), who were killed on 25 August 1922 at Whitehall in north Dublin by Oriel House men; it was widely speculated at the time that they had been killed in direct reprisal for the death of Collins himself the previous week. And Squad member Charlie Dalton was widely implicated in the killings of three other Fianna Éireann boys who were arrested on 21 November 1922 for putting up anti-Free State posters, and discovered shot dead at Clondalkin in west Dublin the following day.

The new government was relatively untroubled by such democratic institutions as courts and inquests: the emergency legislation now on the statute books gave the authorities the liberty to rule as it saw fit. On 1 November 1922, the Dáil adjourned for a fortnight in order, as Patrick Hogan euphemistically had it, to give the government 'a free hand to restore order'. What this meant in practice was that, on 17 November, four rank-and-file IRA men – Peter Cassidy, John Gaffney,

James Fisher and Richard Twohig, who had been caught in possession of revolvers, were executed under the catch-all banner of 'military necessity'. This was the term used by Mulcahy in response to questions from the Labour Party (in effect the opposition party of the new state), which had been shocked to discover that the first intimation they had of executions came only with the news that they had been carried out. Kevin O'Higgins made no bones about justifying the executions, stating publicly that the four young men selected for death had been chosen because if they had begun the executions with someone 'outstandingly wicked', people might have thought it was out of simple vengeance or because he was an Englishman.

The following week, the execution of the 'outstandingly wicked' Englishman took place. Erskine Childers was arrested at Glendalough in County Wicklow, found guilty of being in possession of a revolver, and shot at dawn at Beggars Bush barracks in Dublin on 24 November 1922. The revolver in question had been given to him by Michael Collins – and Childers is remembered for the calm manner in which he went to his death. On the eve of his execution, for example, he warned his son Erskine (who would one day become President of Ireland) never to bear hatred against his father's killers.

On the morning of his execution he asked for and was granted a delay in proceedings until the light improved, so that the firing squad could be sure of killing him outright. He shook hands with each member of his firing squad; he asked not to be blindfolded, but his request was refused – and after his eyes were bandaged, he stood to attention before being shot dead.

In all, the execution proceedings took an hour and fifteen minutes from the time he was brought from his cell. A few days after Childers was shot, three more prisoners were executed at Beggars Bush barracks. Joseph Spooner, Patrick Farrelly and John Murphy had been captured near Oriel House in possession of revolvers and bombs after an unsuccessful effort had been made to blow up the building. It is difficult to avoid the conclusion that in the climate of the time, the subsequent killings conducted by former members of the Squad under the banner of Oriel House, were all part and parcel of unacknowledged government policy.

Many decades later, a defence of these policies from an unlikely quarter was given to me. It came from Vivion de Valera, de Valera's eldest son, and himself a proponent of the death penalty. Vivion claimed that his father had said to him on more than one occasion, 'Viv, if it weren't for the executions, the civil war would still be going on.' Vivion de Valera was speaking at the height of the Troubles in Northern Ireland – and, of course, many years after his father had conducted executions of his own during the Second World War.

In terms of *Realpolitik*, de Valera was probably correct; but in the Dáil, Mulcahy defended such executions in terms that revealed the implacable Catholic conscience of the majority of the cabinet – in words that might just as easily have been uttered in the days of the Spanish Inquisition.

These men who were executed this morning were perhaps uneducated illiterate men, never meaning perhaps to get

into a situation like this, men of no political convictions
perhaps [...] we provided for these men all the spiritual
assistance we could muster to help them in their passage to
eternity. [...] We are people who realise that man is made
in the image and likeness of God and we treat man as such
[...] When a man is going to his death he does get a priest.

Such executions, however, did not go unanswered by the Anti-
Treaty forces. After the emergency powers legislation was
passed by the government sanctioning the death penalty for
those caught bearing arms illegally, Liam Lynch – who was
commanding the Anti-Treaty forces – issued a proclamation
calling for the shooting of any TD who voted for the legislation. This fell proclamation set in train a horrible sequence of
events, which exemplifies the entire tragedy of the Irish Civil
War. On 6 December 1922, the Pro-Treaty TD Seán Hales –
a former close associate of Collins and (in an example of the
bitter divisions that characterised the Civil War) a brother of
Tom Hales, who was one of the leaders of the ambush that
killed Collins – was shot dead by Anti-Treaty forces, and his
companion Pádraic Ó Máille seriously wounded.

The government reacted ferociously. It was thought that
Hales's death was the precursor to a general onslaught on the
cabinet and members of the government. In fact, it was discovered many years later by the writer Ulick O'Connor (during
the production of his highly successful play *Executions*) that
the shooting was the individual action of a young Anti-Treaty
Volunteer named Owen Donnelly, who had thought it his duty

to act on Liam Lynch's proclamation. He duly reported his action to his superior officer Seán Caffrey, who, over half a century later, attended the first night of O'Connor's play and told the author what had happened.

This information, had it come to light earlier, might have averted one of the most awful crimes of the period: the murder of Noel Lemass after the Civil War had ended. Lemass was a brother of Seán Lemass, who had been active with the Squad on Bloody Sunday, and would later become Ireland's most effective Taoiseach. Noel Lemass, like his brother, was active on the Anti-Treaty side: he was kidnapped in June 1923 and murdered, and his body was eventually found in the Dublin Mountains in a condition better imagined than described. It was never established exactly who was responsible for the torture and killing of Lemass, but David Neligan himself told me that it was the 'Tobin bunch'. Noel Lemass had been a gifted intelligence officer with the Anti-Treaty Dublin Brigade IRA; he had been suspected of intercepting correspondence between Michael Collins and his fiancée Kitty Kiernan. To some Collins devotees, this alone night have seemed grounds for execution in the fervid political atmosphere of the day. However, the general belief was that Lemass was murdered because it was thought he was responsible for the Hales and Ó Máille shootings.

In revenge for the killing of Seán Hales, and to demonstrate its resolve, the cabinet now decided to execute four prominent Anti-Treaty figures who, having been captured months earlier and imprisoned ever since, could have had nothing whatever to do with the shooting of Hales but were chosen rather to make an impact on their supporters and because they came from each of the four provinces. These four men were Rory O'Connor, Joe McKelvey, Dick Barrett and Liam Mellows. O'Connor had been Kevin O'Higgins's best man: he went to his death with two gold sovereigns sewn into his clothing which had been given to him by O'Higgins as a wedding gift. Now, O'Higgins himself signed the execution warrant for O'Connor and his comrades. The four men were executed in Mountjoy Jail by firing squad at dawn on 8 December. These were executions that, even in the frightful climate of the time, caused wide-spread public shock and consternation.

In a spirit of fairness to the Free State government and its ministers, it should be noted that it had earlier taken a resolute line *against* reprisal executions at the time of Collins's death, when there was considerable pressure from his old army col-leagues to retaliate. Vinnie Byrne told me himself that after Béal na Bláth, most of Collins's men would have shot de Valera if they could have got near him – such was the spirit of bitterness abroad in the land at this time. This verdict was endorsed by Joseph McGrath with whom I conducted an interview, the most fascinating portions of which were unfortunately off the record. McGrath told me that he had to make special arrangements to ensure that de Valera was not attacked 'because there were a lot of fellows around at the time to whom a life didn't mean much'.

Nowhere during the Civil War was the lack of discipline on the part of former Squad members more evident than in County Kerry. As we have already seen, the people of Kerry (and in particular, the inhabitants of Tralee) had already been scourged during the Black and Tan era. Kerry people make the best friends and worst enemies in Ireland – perhaps because comparative geographical isolation has fostered a certain distinctiveness of character. This was summed up for me by a Kerry Maynooth professor whom I asked for an explanation as to why Listowel produced so many writers and top civil servants. He replied, 'Simple, boy: high mountains and good teachers!' It is certainly the case that the members of the Kerry Brigade of the IRA were almost unanimous in opposing the Treaty. Consequently the Kerry IRA initially fought far harder against the Free State forces than they had against the Black and Tans.

By the time the authorities descended on Kerry, the IRA in the county was led by the aggressive and strong-willed Humphrey Murphy. In July 1922, Murphy delivered a speech in Tralee at a meeting called to achieve peace. He said:

> If the Provisional government continue to fight with English guns, English bullets and shells, English armoured cars and the ex-soldiers of the English army […] I am certain that they are going to fail as the Black and Tans failed, because the war did not come properly until it came to Cork and Kerry. We will defend every town to the last. You will have towns in ruins and famine facing those who have escaped the bullet. We will stop at nothing and we are going to win, even if it takes years.

Very shortly thereafter, the war which up to then had largely been confined to Dublin *did* come to Kerry. Emmet Dalton devised a scheme of seaborne landings which took the IRA in Cork and Kerry completely by surprise – but the IRA in Kerry retaliated with a series of drastic measures aimed at implementing Humphrey Murphy's doctrine. In the two months after the Free State troops landed, thirty-five government soldiers were killed – the same number as the total number of RIC fatalities in the county for the entire Anglo-Irish war.

Murphy's men asked for, and gave, no quarter. On 2 August 1922, members of the medical corps treating wounded comrades in Tralee were fired on – despite the fact that a Red Cross flag was being flown. This tactic continued throughout the war, and reached a nadir when two off-duty medics punting on one of Killarney's picturesque lakes were shot dead, despite their Red Cross insignia. Murphy's men also fired on troops guarding food convoys attempting (ultimately successfully) to bring food to towns where provisions were scarce.

Among the most heinous in this flurry of crimes were the killings by Anti-Treaty forces of two of their fellow Kerrymen, the Scarteen O'Connor brothers Tom (aged 20) and John (24) who were both serving and very efficient Free State army officers. The men who carried out the killings, at Kenmare in September 1922, were described as a group of 'maverick' Republicans by historian Tom Doyle, who points out that some of them in fact wore Free State uniforms. It is certainly the case that this force shot the two young brothers in very dubious and ugly circumstances: in a night raid on their home, the IRA unit killed the unarmed John as he came downstairs to investigate the intrusion; Tom, meanwhile, was dragged from his bed and shot. One aspect of this episode is especially chilling: it was not so much the O'Connor brothers' Free State activities per se that led to their deaths, as the fact that their killers regarded them as renegades because of their support of the Dublin-based authorities; the brothers, in other words, appeared to have been targeted largely because they were helping the 'outsiders'. Now a spate of extra-judicial killings broke out all over Kerry. Such vendetta killings became all too common on both sides.

Bitter confrontation continued in Kerry throughout that winter of 1922–23, but the month of March 1923 produced the worst atrocities of all – when gelignite entered the exchange. First, on 6 March 1923, the explosion of a mine at the townland of Knocknagoshel, north-east of Tralee, claimed the lives of five Free State soldiers. Two of them, Captains Michael Dunne and Joseph Stapleton, were prominent Dublin guardsmen; Stapleton, indeed, was a particular friend of Paddy Daly. Over eighty years later, I visited the evil spot with two Kerry friends, Jo Jo Barrett and John O'Mahony, who were both staunch Republicans. Barrett had researched the Knocknagoshel episode for his book *In the Name of the Game*; John O'Mahony is a noted collector of Republican documents, and is the author of *Frongoch*, the standard work on the post-1916 Rising prisoners who were interned in north Wales.

If ever a place had bad karma, this was it. At the time, there was nothing to mark the spot where the mine exploded: a memorial has since been erected, though it was quickly vandalised. Instead, the scene of the atrocity is a nondescript spot: a small field slopes down to a little river, with around it the remnants of Barranarig Wood; and scattered about the place are stones dating from the time of the atrocity. Barrett has described the area as being 'scenic and peaceful'; I, however, found it redolent of a violent history, and speedily left the place. People in the area are still sensitive about the Knocknagoshel incident – which was, after all, not merely attributable to Civil War hostilities, but also redolent of peasant cunning, war between neighbours, deep-seated vengeance and the brooding character of bruised souls, reared in a milieu of foggy mountains, dark nights and dark tales told and retold.

This is not mere fancy on my part. In *In the Name of the Game*, Jo Jo Barrett gives a well-researched, objective account of what transpired – and he shows that local antagonisms did play a part in the story. The local IRA became suspicious of a farmer, Patrick O'Connor, after a number of their local personnel were captured, and planned ambushes discovered and thwarted. The IRA sent one of their men, a Patrick Buckley, to the O'Connor farm in the uniform of a Free State officer; O'Connor duly fell for the impersonation, and willingly passed on information to the imposter. O'Connor was fined by the Republicans: he refused to pay; and his cattle were seized, along with his pony and trap. The IRA party which seized O'Connor's cattle, however, was seen and recognised by his son, Pat, who retaliated by joining the Free State Army the following day. He was rapidly made an officer, and speedily acquired a reputation for maltreating prisoners. Helped by his local knowledge, the junior O'Connor became the scourge of the Knocknagoshel IRA, members of which were forced to leave their homes and sleep rough because of the raids he led. Almost inevitably, a retributive plot was laid.

A local schoolteacher, Kathleen Walsh, was induced to write a note, giving details of an alleged hide and arms dump in Barranarig Wood. (In order to disguise her handwriting, the teacher wrote the note with her left hand.) The note was then given to a schoolgirl to deliver to a sentry at nearby Castleisland barracks. The note led the Free State authorities to believe that the refuge in the woods was the hiding-place both of Humphrey Murphy and of another Republican leader, Mick McGlynn. In fact, it contained a mine which had been brought on a bicycle from twelve miles away in a schoolbag strapped to the crossbar. Unknowingly, a large party of Free State soldiers arrived at Knocknagoshel on 6 March, and surrounded the hide. While examining a cairn of stones which they took to be its entrance, they triggered the mine. The explosion claimed five lives: those of three local men, including Pat O'Connor, and the two Dubliners Dunne and Stapleton. A few weeks later, a brother of the man who made the mine was taken to the field in Knocknagoshel where the mine had exploded; twenty-three bullets were fired into his body.

Horrifying as this sequence of events certainly was, it constituted but a small part of the tale of Civil War horrors at Knocknagoshel. Jo Jo Barrett interviewed Michael Walsh, the nephew of the man who had made the Knocknagoshel mine – and heard from him the details of the ripple effects of the mine explosion in the wider family. Michael Walsh's aunt, Kathleen Walsh (the teacher who had written the fatal note), and her three sisters were all captured by Free State soldiers: they were tortured and had their heads shaved. They all emigrated. Kathleen Walsh's life, indeed, was probably saved by the fact that, when forced to give a sample of her handwriting, she was able to exonerate herself by using her right hand. Buckley, who had impersonated a Free State officer, was one of those murdered in other reprisals for Knocknagoshel. As Michael Walsh told Barrett, the explosion of the mine 'wrecked our family through emigration and death'.

In fact, as we shall see, it led to far more 'wrecking' even than that.

CHAPTER ELEVEN

'Honeycombed with Factions'

The Irish Free State cabinet, October 1922: left to right, Joseph McGrath, Hugh Kennedy, William T. Cosgrave (President of the Executive Council), Ernest Blythe, Kevin O'Higgins and J. J. Walsh.

T HE ASSASSINATION PHILOSOPHY OF THE SQUAD ORDAINED
that not merely was an eye for an eye justifiable, but that
the taking of the enemy's entire head was permissible. For
several months before the Kerry campaign, the Squad had been
to some degree rudderless, missing Collins's control as much as
his presence. Collins's policy, that shooting was a disagreeable
necessity to be used with discrimination, did not now transfer
to Kerry. After Knocknagoshel, much worse was to come – as
both Daly and Neligan reacted with fury to events in the south-
west. Daly said later of his Kerry sojourn, 'No one told me to
bring any kid gloves, so I didn't bring any.' It was due to his
lack of kid gloves, then, that he introduced a new policy against
the remnant of the Anti-Treaty faction: he authorised the use of
Republican prisoners to clear allegedly mined roads because it
was 'the only alternative left us to prevent the wholesale
slaughter of our men'.

The policy was translated into action on 7 March 1923, the
day after Knocknagoshel. Nine Republican prisoners were taken
from Ballymullen barracks in Tralee to Ballyseedy crossroads,
just outside the town, and set to work to remove a barricade
which had been mined. The men appeared to have been first
tied together when the mine exploded – and the effects were

lethal. Survivors of the initial blast were machine-gunned: nine men in total died; and it was at first thought that there were no survivors. The Free State soldiers gathered up the remains and placed them in coffins which were then sealed. But the relatives opened the coffins and when the mangled contents were revealed, extraordinary and long-remembered scenes of frenzy and grief exploded in Tralee. Then it transpired that one of the prisoners, Stephen Fuller, was blown into a nearby field by the explosion – and lived to tell the tale. As Fuller later became a deputy representing de Valera's Fianna Fáil party, it can be understood why his Civil War experiences helped to fuel the bitterness of Dáil exchanges for years after the war had ended.

In the days and weeks following these events at Knocknagoshel, mass round-ups of suspected Republicans were commonplace. Torture was the order of the day as Daly and Neligan sought information on their opponents. I remember Neligan as a civilised and courteous man who taught me to smoke cigars as he did: with a good cigar, he told me, a lighted match should always be passed along its length, so that the leaf expands and provides a better smoke. Neligan was also one of the best raconteurs I ever knew, denoting the passage of time in the retelling of historical events by drawing his right arm across his forehead, and saying, 'Many years passed over our heads, and then...' This, however, is not how Neligan is recalled by Republicans in Kerry. He was accustomed to interrogating prisoners at Hartnett's Hotel at Castleisland: and there are allegations that what he did there was on a par with anything engaged in by the British inside the cells of Dublin Castle. It is certainly the case that the series of events connected with the Knocknagoshel mine only intensified Neligan's activities. In her *Tragedies of Kerry* (1924), Dorothy Macardle described what happened on the night before Ballyseedy:

> 'Interrogation' by Neligan in Ballymullen Barracks was an ordeal under which reason might give way. The prisoner, in the usual practice, was first blindfolded, then his arms were tied to his sides, and 'interrogation' began. This time a hammer was used. The prisoners were taken in separately. When [John] Shanahan came out his head was covered with blood and his spine was injured, but he was still able to walk. The hammer failed. The prisoners were taken out to be shot, and shots were fired round their heads. They were then sentenced, for their obdurate silence, to be executed at midnight and were then locked in their cells.

Shanahan's ordeal probably saved his life, because his injuries meant that he was not taken out with the other Ballyseedy victims to the mined barricade the following morning. This, however, was the only good thing one can say about Neligan's methods in Kerry, which unfortunately were not confined to the night before Ballyseedy.

The Bahaghs incident – or Cahirciveen incident, as it is more properly known – occurred five days after Ballyseedy, on 12 March 1923. A military court presided over by Paddy Daly convened on 7 April: it heard evidence from a Commandant Delany that he had taken five prisoners from the workhouse in Bahaghs in the early hours of 12 March to remove a barricade on the road between Cahirciveen and Valentia, about a mile from Bahaghs workhouse. Delany claimed that he had inspected the barricade but did not see the mine. He denied that the prisoners were shot, and denied too that he and his party had been heard boasting in a bar at Cahirciveen about the killings after the explosion; he said that, on the contrary, neither he nor his party had entered a bar. The finding of the court was that no blame could be attached to any officer or soldier engaged in the operations in which these prisoners lost their lives. The court's verdict was that 'in view of the abnormal conditions which had prevailed in this area and of the inordinate and malignant nature of the fight carried out against the Army in their efforts to restore Peace, the discipline maintained by the troops is worthy of the highest consideration'.

Similar findings were issued on the Ballyseedy explosion, and on a second explosion on the same day at Countess Bridge in Killarney, in which four Republican prisoners died. However, my father Eamonn Coogan has left a different account of what transpired, which gives the lie to the finding of the military court. He was at the time Deputy Commissioner of the new Garda Síochána police force: and he investigated the Kerry deaths following a compensation case taken by Maurice Riordan, the father of eighteen-year-old William Riordan who was one of the Bahaghs victims. Maurice Riordan was described by my father in his report – held in the archives of the Irish Department of Justice and released to the public in 2008 – as 'being in needy circumstances': he goes on to remark that the elder Riordan blamed his son's death on 'members of the National Army known as the "Visiting Committee" who removed William from the Bahaghs workhouse and killed him by dragging him over a mine on the public road'. My father found that the facts stated by Maurice Riordan were true: that William Riordan, 'an Irregular and one of a column captured with arms' was taken from temporary imprisonment at Bahaghs workhouse and 'done to death' with four other prisoners by the 'Visiting Committee' – a much-feared body of worthies which went from barracks to barracks, selecting prisoners for execution.

In those circumstances, I would like to think that I would have shown the courage to compile such a report in similar circumstances, but I doubt it. However, not only was the report not acted on: the Riordans, who lived at or below the breadline, in fact received no compensation. The cabinet decided that 'evidence of complicity in an attack against the State on the part of an applicant for compensation or in respect of whom compensation is claimed is a bar to the claim'. This mean-spirited and ungenerous approach was followed in all the cases involving victims of the Kerry explosions. What this policy meant in practice may be deduced from what my father wrote about the widow and six children of Patrick Buckley, who was killed in the aftermath of Knocknagoshel. Of these my father wrote: 'they have no visible means of obtaining a livelihood.'

My father – although he was the highest ranking official – was not the *only* Free State supporter to reveal what happened in Kerry. A National Army lieutenant named Niall Harrington, who later became a respected figure in Irish business circles, took the unusually courageous step of going to Dublin in person to inform the authorities of what was happening in Kerry at that time. He received an apparently sympathetic hearing – but incredibly was sent back to Kerry to the same barracks in which he was stationed. A bullet missed his head by inches on the night he returned, and he sat up all night with two revolvers in hand. But equally incredibly, his reposting turned out to have been an error rather than a murderous tactic. Harrington survived and later wrote a book about his experiences.

Another army officer, a Lieutenant McCarthy, reported of the Bahaghs atrocity that the five men were '*murdered* [my italics] on the road this morning'. But the official army communiqué on the atrocity read, as Macardle relates in her *Tragedies of Kerry*: 'There was no ambush in the vicinity; all our troops had been removed from Cahirciveen and the workhouse. There was no barricade and no mine laid there by us. The five prisoners had been arrested by us more than a week earlier.' It was, then, not only the horrible atrocities themselves which generated hatred and long-lasting emotions in Kerry and throughout the country, but also the extreme callousness with which the authorities in general behaved towards the people.

One of the allegations made in Kerry about Neligan in particular is that he carefully selected those who were to be killed, screening them to ensure that they did not have – for example – clerical or other influential relations in their family, who might be able to generate investigations into what happened. But the events at Clashmealcon caves, located on cliffs in north

County Kerry near the mouth of the Shannon, do not indicate any respect or concern for the activities of clergy. Here a group of Republicans held out against a siege by Free State soldiers for three days and nights, in the process withstanding attempts to smoke them out using straw and tar. One of the group, Timothy 'Aero' Lyons, fell to his death when a rope on which he was being hauled to the cliff edge either broke, or was cut. Either way, his death was guaranteed: he was fired on where he lay. Two other cave inmates who attempted to scale the cliffs slipped and were drowned. Amongst the survivors was Jim McEnery, whose brother Tom, a priest, returned from Britain after the capture of the Clashmealcon survivors. The cleric spent a day and a night telephoning Daly trying to find out news of his brother and the other prisoners. Eventually Daly sent a reply, assuring the priest that the group 'will be executed when we have time'. Sure enough, a few days later the prisoners were duly shot. Such memories ensured that the Republican tradition in the south-west remains strong to the present day.

There is nothing glorious about such tales – and it is neither pleasant nor honourable for Michael Collins's Squad to have been involved in the events that spawned them. In addition, such shameful episodes did not end even with the conclusion of the Civil War. The sense of victimisation felt by many influential Free State cabinet members and other figures – encapsulated in Kevin O'Higgins's famous remark that 'the Provisional Government was simply eight young men in the City Hall standing amidst the ruins of one administration with the foundations of another not yet laid, and with wild men screaming through the keyhole' – ensured that ugly episodes were able to continue, and to continue to be covered up. Another major cover-up, indeed, occurred after a scandalous incident directly involving Paddy Daly – and it also took place in Kerry.

At 1am on 22 June 1923 – that is, after the Civil War had officially ended – three men knocked on the door of Dr Randal McCarthy, a general practitioner in Kenmare. They announced that they were members of the military, and were duly admitted. Once in the house, the men dragged McCarthy's two daughters Florence (generally known as Flossie) and Jessie into the garden by their hair, in their nightgowns, and beat them with their Sam Browne belts. Flossie gave evidence that as her sister lay on the ground, one man stood on her to enable the others to beat her. After the girls had been beaten, the men rubbed thick motor oil into their hair. The men were later identified as Daly himself, plus a 'Captain Flood' and a 'Captain Clarke'. Amongst the evidence heard by a military enquiry held in O'Connor barracks at Kenmare a week later was the fact that a Colt revolver was left behind by one of the assailants. This model was one of the weapons of choice used by the Squad, a fact which may or may not have been of significance. However, the fact that the court was told that the butt of the weapon had a series of marks ('scratches', as they were described) on it, makes one wonder if they were indeed scratches – or notches.

The motivation for the attack has been attributed to the fact that the McCarthy girls had been friendly with British officers – although the McCarthy home had been a safe house for Volunteers during the Anglo-Irish war – and that one of them was said to have spurned the affections of a Free State officer. Whatever the motive, there is no doubt that the officer commanding the Free State troops in Kerry, plus two of his officers, had been involved in a shameful incident. However, when Cahir Davitt, the army's Judge Advocate General, was summoned to the office of Commander in Chief Richard Mulcahy, he was informed that Mulcahy had interviewed Daly personally; had asked him, man to man, whether he was involved in the McCarthy affair; and had been assured that he was not. Mulcahy said that, given Daly's distinguished 'military and national record, that it would be deplorable if he were put to the necessity of defending himself of the charge before a Court Martial'. Mulcahy maintained that attitude subsequently, and as Davitt records, the disgraceful business never became public. There was, in fact, some limited publicity about a year later, when the Labour leader Thomas Johnson raised the matter in the Dáil; but as the young McCarthy women never took a civil action, the matter was largely hushed up – although it was certainly widely spoken of in Kerry. The latitude shown to the former Squad leader, however, had a bearing on the final great crisis involving the surviving Apostles.

*

At this point, I want to digress for a necessary moment to refer to Collins's attitude to the new state of Northern Ireland, its governance, and the political philosophy of its founding Unionist elite. It is virtually certain that one of Collins's

objectives in promoting his incremental or 'stepping-stone' attitude to the Treaty – his main justification, in other words, for
accepting the Treaty in its imperfect state – was that he foresaw
in due course the ending of the partition of Ireland. His close
friend and fellow IRB member Seán Hales is remembered as
having told friends that Collins intended to use the Treaty as
a step towards full independence, remarking that 'The English
broke the Treaty of Limerick [that is, the accord which ended
the seventeenth-century Williamite Wars in Ireland, and which
led to land seizures and the Penal Laws] and we'll break this
Treaty.' Certainly Hales is on the record of arguing in favour
of the Treaty at a time when the vote for it hung in the balance.
He claimed, on 17 December 1921, that when 'the army of
occupation' was withdrawn:

> In a short time with the building-up of the youth of the
> country, the training of their minds and the training of
> them as soldiers and the equipping, that day will soon be at
> hand when you could place Ireland to my mind in rightful
> place amongst the Nations of the Earth [...] When Sarsfield
> under duress signed that Treaty with the English King,
> foolishly enough [...] he honourably kept his word and they
> honourably broke it. Well the day is coming when we will
> pay that back. There is no fear that the soul of Ireland will
> die. Ireland's destiny is to be a Republic.

Hales made these comments during the fraught Dáil debates
on the Treaty – and it was noted that Collins did not repudiate

him. Collins was certainly outraged by the treatment of the Catholic minority in the new Northern Ireland: it was for this reason, as we have seen, that he almost certainly ordered the assassination of Sir Henry Wilson. But he was also determined as a matter of principle to see a thirty-two-county Ireland, as envisaged in the 1916 Rising. He created a number of initiatives to bring this about, which were in flagrant breach of the Treaty and completely at odds with the attitude of the bulk of his cabinet colleagues towards the issue of Partition. One such policy – and one which died with him – was the paying of the salaries of Nationalist schoolteachers in Northern Ireland so that they would subvert the Unionist curriculum of teaching only British history and in general disparaging Irish culture.

Another, highly audacious, ploy was to kidnap, in February 1922, forty-two Orangemen in Counties Derry, Fermanagh and Tyrone, spirit them across the highly porous Irish border and hide them in Free State barracks across the south of the country. These individuals could then be held as bargaining chips – specifically to ensure the safety of IRA personnel due to be executed at Derry Jail; these men were subsequently reprieved. The kidnappings caused consternation in ruling Unionist circles in the North – and across the water too, where a startled Lloyd George, then in the final months of his premiership, was kept fully apprised of events.

But his most deadly policy – literally speaking – was to arm members of the IRA in the Six Counties. These weapons found their way circuitously across the border: Collins struck a deal for such goods to pass from the Anti-Treaty IRA in the Free State into the hands of the IRA in Northern Ireland; the weapons store of the Anti-Treaty IRA was then replenished with guns not traced back to Collins. Such a deal was complex, ingenious and laced with irony – but it served a vital function too, for the contraband weaponry now in circulation north of the border could never be traced back to Collins himself.

Such measures were part of much larger campaign meditated by Collins. One of the leaders of this campaign was Roger McCorley, who, noting how the relationship between Collins and the British had deteriorated steadily in the period leading up to the shelling of the Four Courts in June 1922, wrote:

> It was decided that a big effort be made to bring about, if possible, the downfall of the Six-County government by military means and various offensive actions were planned. This operation was decided on in Dublin at a meeting at which an Army executive from the Four Courts, GHQ Portobello and divisional commanders from the Six Counties were present.

Collins had not empowered the GHQ representatives to be present at the meeting with promised military equipment for the offensive, simply for reasons of conspiratorial duplicity. Quite apart from the fact that he sincerely believed in a united Ireland at that point in the summer of 1922, he was also desperately trying to hold the two wings of the IRA together: those responsive to GHQ and to himself who supported the

Treaty, and those in what had become known as the IRA Army Executive who supported the Four Courts men. Backing the IRA in support of the beleaguered Nationalists in Northern Ireland both postponed a split and furthered the 'stepping-stone' policy.

The Northern campaign was short-lived, intense and bloody. The forces of the Northern Ireland government – including a partisan police force, various 'Special Corps' (whom Lloyd George described as the 'fascisti') plus a heavy British military presence – and the enmity of a majority of the population, together proved too strong for even a united IRA. It is worth noting just how ruthless was the response of the authorities: armed B-Special units and other undercover agents invaded Catholic districts, shooting civilians under the cover of darkness – and setting off further cycles of reprisal. McCorley describes how one of these Protestant gangs was dealt with:

> I had issued a general order that where reprisal gangs were cornered no prisoners were to be taken. The enemy, after a short time, offered to surrender, but our men, in obedience to the order, refused to accept their surrender. The fight continued for about forty minutes and only finished when the last of the reprisal gang was wiped out.

As it happened, McCorley was one of those who subsequently brought their ruthless expertise to bear while fighting for the Free State in the Civil War. When the campaign was called off in August 1922, McCorley was one of the officers who accepted Collins's word that it would be resumed once the Civil War had ended. Speaking at Dublin's Portobello Barracks on 1 August (just a few weeks before he was killed) Collins specifically told the officers: 'The Civil War will be over in a few weeks. Then we can resume in the North. You men will get special training.' Henceforth, for the few remaining weeks of his life, the successful prosecution of the Civil War would become Collins's first priority. But it should be pointed out that not only were the Northern Ireland IRA leaders whom he summoned to Dublin informed that the cessation of the campaign in the Six Counties was only temporary, and would last only for the duration of the Civil War – the Crow Street cadre and at least some members of the Squad believed this also.

*

While Collins's Northern strategy had run into the sand, events in the Free State were continuing to unfold – and in the aftermath of his death, the greater game continued. In particular, such scandals as occurred at Kenmare would have wider political implications, though these would take time to play out. The ruthless Kevin O'Higgins valued discipline in the ranks, and as the Civil War came to an end, he vowed to use the Kenmare incident as leverage to drive Mulcahy from the cabinet. The result was a storm that would have implications North and South of the border. Some of these implications can be glimpsed in a letter (held today by the National Library of Ireland) of 7 August 1923 from Major General James Hogan,

Director of Intelligence to General Seán Mac Mahon, Chief of General Staff. Hogan wrote that:

> Today the Army from top to bottom is honeycombed with factions, and factionalism is killing discipline and efficiency. Much of this sectionalism is formless but an amount is the result of premeditation [...] Officers from the Viceregal Lodge have convened meetings in Dublin and have had in attendance officers – junior and senior – from all over the country. These officers are being asked to sit in judgement on the question of army control and on their brother officers. They have constituted themselves a final court of appeal.

Hogan went on to link the Kenmare situation to the trouble brewing in the Army:

> The attention of the Army has been focused in this incident for some time. [...] I was informed that officers of my own staff dare not investigate the affair and give justice [and] that officers from the Kerry command have been in Dublin canvassing officers for their support of the GOC Kerry [...] One of these officers is Colonel Joe Leonard [...] if the affair is let lapse it will be construed by many as a sign of weakness and you can be assured that these elements will then take the bit in their mouth with a vengeance [...] I believe that the future of the army is in great measure bound up with the strict doing of Justice.

The reference to 'Viceregal officers' was code for Squad members Tobin and Cullen, who had been appointed aides de camp to the Governor General Tim Healy. They were spearheading what can only be termed a mutinous movement within the Army, which was caused by a number of factors. One was resentment at an attempt to reorganise the IRB as a force within the Army, which would both offset their influence and play a role in deciding who should stay and who should go. This in turn was part of a wider post-conflict movement 'downsizing' the army from a total of 60,000 men to which it had mushroomed during the Civil War, to a far smaller unit tailored to the needs of the new peace-time era.

The 'mutineers' were not solely motivated by anger at the shrinking of the Army, though one of their claims was that too many ex-British soldiers and officers were being retained in its ranks, to the detriment of people like themselves who had actually fought the British. Ideologically speaking, however, the *general* grievance was one which may be traced back to Michael Collins himself – and specifically his attitude to Northern Ireland. This was that the new Free State government had now abandoned Collins's 'stepping-stone' policy: instead, it was solely concerned with consolidating the Free State itself, thus abandoning the North and accepting the fact of Partition. Indeed, they were perfectly correct. It would be fair to say that almost as soon as Collins's funeral service had ended, the Free State cabinet ended his interventionist policy in the North. The border, far from vanishing in the years to come, would remain intact and embedded in the fabric of Irish life. But in those early days, this future could not be foreseen: and even if the cabinet in general set its face against intervention, there remained elements within it, as well as within the Army and the remnants of the Squad, who continued to favour intervention and the end to Partition.

Matters came to a head (although the public were not aware of it at the time) on 7 March 1924, when Tobin and his fellow mutineers served an ultimatum on the government, demanding an end to demobilisations and the suspension of the Army Council. The mutineers had drawn up some drastic action plans, including the kidnapping of cabinet members' families – although it is quite likely that these were known to O'Higgins through his intelligence operatives. Orders, then, were given to proceed against the mutineers: and on 16 March, after delays in the senior army command (although these stopped short of active resistance), Devlin's public house in Dublin's north inner city – as we know, a favoured meeting place of the Squad – was surrounded by troops. The mutineers were arrested, though not before Joe McGrath was allowed to buy them a drink.

However, no courts martial followed. A combination of McGrath's diplomacy, and respect for the records of Tobin, Cullen, Dalton, Thornton, Joe Dolan and other participants in this attempted mutiny, meant that the situation was defused diplomatically. The mutineers accepted the principle of civilian control over the army; and arms which the mutineers had secretly requisitioned were returned. McGrath and others who had supported the Tobin faction resigned from the government; later, they formed their own short-lived political party, which they named the National Party. O'Higgins was able at last to vent his long-standing antipathy toward Mulcahy: he was dismissed from the cabinet, and did not regain his position in national life until 1927 – and then only after three IRA men had removed O'Higgins from the scene by means of assassination.

A welter of other sackings and resignations now took place within the Army. Some of these were clearly unjust, and were enforced on senior officers who had managed to keep a dangerous situation under control by exerting restraint towards the Tobin group, while at the same time curbing mutinous tendencies within the Army itself. In all, as I note in my *Ireland in the Twentieth Century*, the mutiny claimed the resignations of 'two ministers, three major generals, seven colonels, nearly thirty commandants, forty captains and nineteen lieutenants'. The episode itself put a definitive end to the influence of the IRB. What was left of their finances helped to defray the cost of erecting a monument to Wolfe Tone, the father of modern Irish Republicanism: this was commissioned as part of the 1966 commemoration of the Easter Rising, and placed on St Stephen's Green. (This was blown up by Ulster Loyalists in 1971, and repaired subsequently.) Among the resignations, meanwhile, was that of Major General Patrick Daly: and so the Kenmare incident vanished into history with no military or criminal charges being brought. Davitt has recorded that when he found that Mulcahy would not bring military law to bear on Daly, he recommended that Hugh Kennedy, the government's chief law officer, bring civil criminal proceedings. But, in a decision more appropriate to a Latin American dictatorship than to the fledgling Irish democracy, Kennedy decided that Daly, who had entered a house under false pretences and flogged two of its residents, had no case to answer.

The mutiny – or proposed mutiny – marked a definitive end to the days of the Twelve Apostles. Events had run their course: the two parts of Ireland were travelling on different roads; and the history of the Free State in which these Apostles lived was now to become one in which hearts and minds would be absorbed by different matters – by money or the lack of it, by emigration, by cultural stagnation, and by a bitter economic war with Britain. Individual members of the Apostles would play their part in the story of these post-Independence years – so let us end by glancing at some of these stories, and observing how these individuals fared.

Afterword

I HAVE TO BEGIN THIS AFTERWORD ON A DISTINCTLY inglorious note – by recording the story of Squad member **Joseph Conroy**. He murdered Emmanuel Kahn, a leading member of Dublin's Jewish community, in November 1923: there had been other shootings of Jews in Dublin at the time; and Conroy's actions gave rise to fears that an anti-Jewish pogrom might be underway in the city. Later, however, it was established that Conroy had been acting on behalf of a friend who was a prostitute, who claimed that Kahn had assaulted her. Conroy fled to the United States in 1925, sensing that the net was closing on him. It has always been assumed that Conroy was aided by David Neligan, who saw to it that the system turned a collective blind eye to the escape.

Joseph McGrath set up the Irish Hospitals Sweepstake in 1930 – and many surviving members of the Squad were employed in what soon became an enormously profitable enterprise. Amongst those who did well were **Charlie Dalton** (whose brother **Emmet** became a film producer), **Joe Dolan** and **Frank Saurin**: indeed, the subsequent enormous success of the Sweepstake organisation was due, in part at least, to the bolstering presence of such figures from the former IRB/Collins network; these individuals had an invaluable part to play in smuggling the proceeds and counterfoils of the Sweepstake in and out of Ireland. McGrath himself became enormously wealthy, and subsequently branched out into many other businesses.

The redoubtable **Vinnie Byrne** fell victim to the Army purges, but ultimately got a job in government service as a carpenter with the Office of Public Works, and became a well-known and popular figure at race meetings. **Patrick Daly** was readmitted to the Army on the outbreak of the Second World War – but only with the rank of Captain and in the construction section; Kenmare, it seemed, was not yet forgotten.

The former Squad leader **Mick McDonnell** prospered in California. He had a son, whom he named Michael Collins, and who served in the United States Air Force. McDonnell became the respected general factotum of the prominent McEnery family headed by John P. McEnery, Superintendent of the United States Mint at San Francisco. McEnery was related to the Jim McEnery who had been executed in Kerry following the Clashmealcon siege – but the American branch of the family knew nothing of such events, and McDonnell remained high in their estimation. The only inkling the family had of McDonnell's Irish activities came when the FBI turned up one day in John P. McEnery's office to complain that McDonnell was selling illegal Irish Sweepstakes tickets. McEnery saw to it that McDonnell was not prosecuted.

Liam Tobin's life took a most curious course. After the mutiny (and although he could not drive), Tobin went into business as a garage owner. He subsequently joined the new Fianna Fáil party, assessing its leader de Valera as the most Republican figure left standing after years of chaos and violence. In later life, Tobin was known to accompany de Valera's wife Sinéad to Mass in south Dublin. Tobin ended his working life as Superintendent of the Dáil, in charge of the security of the parliament that he had done so much both to establish – and to subvert.

Many of the old Squad and Crow Street members became officers in the Army during the Emergency, as the Second World War was euphemistically known in Ireland; and gave loyal service to de Valera in helping to maintain the policy of neutrality. **Tom Cullen** did not long survive the Army mutiny: he died in 1926 in a swimming accident at Lough Dan in his native County Wicklow. **Frank Thornton**, whose personal courage was acknowledged and lauded even by his enemies, became a senior executive in the successful New Ireland Insurance Company.

David Neligan was involved in the establishment of the Irish Special Branch: he modified his interrogation techniques, but was known for eliciting information from suspects by using tactics such as suddenly confronting a recalcitrant with a groaning figure covered in 'blood'; the 'blood' was in fact tomato ketchup. Neligan was fired by de Valera as head of the CID and subsequently spent twenty years, as he said himself, 'trying to find out what he was supposed to be doing' in a non-job in the Department of Lands.

As for **Ned Broy,** whose information had supplied the Squad with so many of their targets: he became Commissioner of the Garda Síochána. The day of the Twelve Apostles was over – but that of the policeman never ends.

A note on sources

THE GROUNDWORK FOR THIS BOOK WAS OF COURSE MY own research for my biography of Michael Collins (1990). This research was carried out in the late 1980s – and has been greatly augmented in the years since by the publication of the Irish Bureau of Military History's personal accounts of the 1916–1921 struggle by those who took part in it. These invaluable documents (with the exception of full accounts from the key figures of Apostles Liam Tobin and Tom Cullen, who died before the Bureau began its work) are now available to the public online at www.bureauofmilitaryhistory.ie.

The eyewitness accounts of the Crow Street and Squad participants in the Irish War of Independence of 1916–1921 are comprehensive. Tobin, who was the central surviving figure of the intelligence war, unfortunately opted for discretion, and his witness statement therefore goes into very little detail about undercover operations. Of those that *do* give full accounts, I have made use of the following: Vinnie Byrne, Bernard C. Byrne, David Neligan, Joe Dolan, James Slattery, Frank Thornton, Joe Leonard, Charles Dalton, Paddy Daly, William J. Stapleton, Mick McDonnell, Daniel McDonnell, Lily Mernin, Frank Saurin, Patrick Caldwell, Patrick Kennedy, Patrick McCrea, Dan Breen, Eamon Broy, Mick Kennedy,

Seamus Robinson, Oscar Traynor, Cahir Davitt and Roger McCorley.

Other primary material used includes:

James Hogan, Director of Intelligence: letter of 7 August 1923 to General S. McMahon.
Private Sessions of Second Dáil. Stationery Office, Dublin.
Proceedings of Court of Enquiry, Kenmare, 26–28 June 1923.

I want to most particularly acknowledge the assistance given to me by Ms. Carmel Kelly, the Librarian, and the staff of the Dalkey Public Library, who used their computer system to secure for me books, both from their own shelves and from libraries all over Ireland.

Select Bibliography

Barrett, J. J., *In the Name of the Game* (Bray: Dub Press, 1997).
Boyne, Seán, *Emmet Dalton* (Dublin: Merrion Press, 2015).
Caulfield, Max, *The Easter Rebellion* (Dublin: Gill & Macmillan, 1963).
Coogan, Tim Pat, *Michael Collins* (London: Hutchinson, 1990).
Coogan, Tim Pat, *De Valera: Long Fellow, Long Shadow* (London: Hutchinson, 1993).
Coogan, Tim Pat, *The IRA* (London: Pall Mall, 1970; subsequently reprinted by HarperCollins, 2002).
Coogan, Tim Pat, *1916: The Easter Rising* (London: Weidenfeld and Nicolson, 2010).
Coogan, Tim Pat, and Morrison, George, *The Irish Civil War: A Photographic Record* (London: Weidenfeld and Nicolson, 1999).

Coogan, Tim Pat, *Ireland Since the Rising* (London: Pall Mall, 1966).

Costello, Francis, *The Irish Revolution* (Dublin: Irish Academic Press, 2003).

Cottrell, Peter, *The Anglo-Irish War* (Oxford: Osprey, 2006).

Doyle, Tom, *The Civil War in Kerry* (Cork: Mercier Press, 2008).

Dwyer, T. Ryle, *The Squad* (Cork: Mercier Press, 2005).

Fanning, Ronan, *The Irish Department of Finance 1922–58* (Dublin: Institute of Public Administration, 1978).

Fanning, Ronan, *Éamon de Valera: A Will to Power* (London: Faber and Faber, 2015)

Foy, Michael T., *Michael Collins's Intelligence War* (Stroud: Sutton Press, 2006).

Hart, Peter (ed.), *Narratives: British Intelligence in Ireland* (Cork: Cork University Press, 2002).

Hittle, J. B. E., *Michael Collins and the Anglo-Irish War: Britain's Counterinsurgency Failure* (Dulles, Virginia: Potomac, 2011).

Litton, Helen *Thomas Clarke* (Dublin: O'Brien Press, 2014).

McMahon, Paul, *British Spies and Irish Rebels* (Martlesham: Boydell Press, 2008).

Murphy, Jeremiah, *When Youth was Mine* (Dublin: Mentor Press, 1998).

Ryan, Meda, *Michael Collins and the Women who Spied for Ireland* (Cork: Mercier Press, 2006).

Valiulis, Maryann, *Portrait of a Revolutionary: General Richard Mulcahy and the Founding of the Irish Free State* (Dublin: Irish Academic Press, 1992).

Yeates, Padráig, *A City in Civil War* (Dublin: Gill & Macmillan, 2015).

Picture credits

Chapter openers

pp. 2–3. Wikimedia Commons; pp. 14–15. Pictorial Press Ltd/
Alamy Stock Photo; pp. 42–3. Wikimedia Commons; pp. 92–3
Wikimedia Commons; pp. 144–5 Topical Press Agency/Getty
Images; pp. 170–1 Topfoto; pp. 195–6 Sean Sexton/Getty
Images; pp. 224–5 Walshe/Getty Images; pp. 254–5 Topfoto;
pp. 276–7 Central Press; Getty Images.

Plate sections

1. Wikimedia Commons; 2. Pictorial Press Ltd/Alamy Stock
Photo; 3. Hulton Archive/Getty Images; 4. Independent News
and Media/Getty Images; 6. Topical Press Agency/Getty Images;
7. National Library of Ireland, Dublin; 9. Pictorial Press Ltd/
Alamy Stock Photo; 13. Walshe/Topical Press Agency/Getty
Images; 14. Wikimedia Commons; 15. Topical Press Agency/
Hulton Archive/Getty Images; 17. Bettman/Getty Images; 18.
Sean Sexton/Getty Images; 19. Topical Press Agency/Getty
Images; 20. Hulton Archive/Getty Images; 21. Hulton Archive/
Getty Images; 22. Hulton Archive/Getty Images; 23. Hulton
Archive/Getty Images; 24. Topical Press Agency/Getty Images;
25. Hulton Archive/Getty Images; 26. Wikimedia Commons;
27. Popperfoto/Getty Images; 28. Hulton Archive/Getty Images;
29. Popperfoto/Getty Images; 30. Central Press/Getty Images;
32. Central Press/Getty Images.

Index

Page references in *italics* indicate illustrations; *fn* indicates a reference to a footnote.